*Monographic Journals of the Near East*     *Afroasiatic Linguistic*

# THE PHONOLOGY OF AKKADIAN SYLLABLE STRUCTURE*

by

**Edward L. Greenstein**
**The Jewish Theological Seminary of America**

The present study adopts a generative theoretical approach and analyzes a number of phonological and morphological rules in Akkadian, especially: *a*-EPENTHESIS, *i*-ADDITION, VOWEL DELETION, VOWEL SHORTENING, VOWEL LENGTHENING, and FEMININE SUFFIX SELECTION. Where necessary, the rules are motivated, described in detail, and reformulated. It is shown that all these rules are subordinated to constraints on Akkadian syllable structure. The Akkadian syllable may have no more than three segments (with the possible exception of a word-final syllable having a long vowel), and phonological rules eliminate overweight syllables, or produce well-formed ones. Sumerian influence seems to have engendered VOWEL DELETION in Akkadian, but the constraints on syllable structure curtail its application. Related issues such as stress, orthography, and Assyrian VOWEL HARMONY are also treated.

## Acknowledgements

This monograph comprises a revision, adaptation, and extension of parts of my Ph.D. Dissertation, completed at Columbia University in 1977. I am indebted to my chief mentor in Semitic philology, Prof. Moshe Held, and my chief mentor in Semitic linguistics, Prof. Joseph L. Malone, as well as the other members of my dissertation committee, Professors Meir M. Bravmann (of blessed memory), David Sperling, and David Marcus, the last of whom deserves special thanks for serving constantly as teacher, sounding board, critic, and friend. I am grateful to the Federal Government, the Danciger Foundation, and Columbia University for fellowships that funded my graduate studies. I owe special thanks to Prof. Giorgio Buccellati of Undena Publications for having encouraged me to extend the context of my dissertation, to sharpen its focus, and to reshape it. Dr. Buccellati's editorial assistants, Matthew Lee Jaffe and

*Textual citations and abbreviations follow Oppenheim et al. (1955- ) (= the Chicago *Assyrian Dictionary*). Note the additional abbreviations: *AAL* for *Afroasiatic Linguistics,* and *LI* for *Linguistic Inquiry.*

John Hayes, were very helpful. And, Prof. William L. Moran has very kindly made some much appreciated corrections and suggestions. If, despite all this assistance and advice, the study is still inadequate, the responsibility is mine alone.

Abridged versions of sections 7 and 8 were presented in 1977 at the annual meetings of the American Oriental Society and the North American Conference on Afroasiatic Linguistics, respectively.

I would like to dedicate this monograph to the memory of my beloved cousin, Walter L. Weisberg.

" ... in der Sprache Alles durch Jedes und Jedes durch Alles bestimmt wird" — Wilhelm von Humboldt.

## Table of Contents

# 1. INTRODUCTION

## 1.1. Rules connected with syllable structure

When we deal with any system of phenomena, we must describe the data by observing them not only in an artificial isolation but also in their natural interaction, in their relations within the system. This is as true of linguistics as it is of anything else. In fact, "The relation of parts and wholes is the fundamental question which faces the science of language in the latter's manifold facets" (Jakobson & Waugh 1979:233, cf. 165-173; Piaget 1970: esp. 74-96). A proper grammar should seek out the various general principles by which a language can be shown to make sense. Accordingly, when one encounters diverse rules of a language which all seem to share a similar function or produce a similar effect, one should look for some common factor to account for these rules (esp. Kisseberth 1970a).

It has been observed in a number of languages, ranging from Tonkawa (Amerindian) to Cairene Arabic, that groups, or "conspiracies," of rules have the effect of breaking up consonant clusters (e.g., Kisseberth 1970a, 1970b, 1972; Kenstowicz & Pyle 1973; Grundt 1976:58; Saib 1978; Broselow 1979; Kenstowicz & Kisseberth 1979:224; Lowenstamm 1981). The dissolution of consonant clusters appears to be not only a widespread phonological process (e.g., Anderson 1973:98; Chambers & Trudgill 1980: 153) but a universal psycholinguistic proclivity as well. For example, children will naturally eliminate consonant clusters from their speech through such devices as consonant reduction (e.g., [say] for *sky*), metathesis (e.g., [nos] for *snow*), and epenthesis (e.g., [bəluw] for *blue)* (Menn 1978). Aphasics will often produce speech errors in which consonant clusters are simplified, as in [pIti] for *pretty* (via reduction) and [hɛlƏp] for *help* (via epenthesis) (Blumstein 1978).

What seems to motivate the dissolution of consonant clusters is constraints on the complexity of syllable structure, a propensity to simplify syllables (cf., e.g., Ingram 1978) or, more positively, to produce preferred syllable types (cf., e.g., Vennemann 1972a; Hooper 1972; Schane 1973a:118-119; Sommerstein 1977:227). Every language has constraints which allow certain sequences of phonemes and disallow others. The syllable often plays a crucial role in the definition of such constraints. For example, English permits stop-liquid sequences at the onset of a syllable but not at its coda; it permits liquid-stop sequences at the coda of a syllable but not at its onset. Thus, we have *blank* but not *lbakn*. The psychological reality of such constraints finds empirical support in experiments in which subjects who were presented with proscribed consonant sequences misperceived them as permissible ones (Cena 1978).

A grammar should identify and describe the phonological constraints of a language and assemble the various rules that are subordinated by these constraints under their heading. One might even say that "The function of phonological rules in general is the conversion of phonetically impermissible structures into phonetically permissible ones" (Iverson and Sanders 1978:11). If so, the phonological rules are, in a sense, agents of these constraints. Consonant clusters are simplified, and well-formed syllables produced, through a number of possible processes: epenthesis of vowels between consonants, deletion of a consonant, reduction of a vowel, insertion of a glide between vowels, affixation of a vowel preceding an initial cluster or following a final cluster. Basically, languages have the option to produce proper syllables either by adding or subtracting segments (cf. Ingria 1980).
The types of procedures by which a language resolves poorly-formed syllables should also become part of its characterization and, therefore, be incorporated into its grammar.

## 1.2. Akkadian rules connected with syllable structure

Two rules of Akkadian phonology are obviously related to syllable structure. The rule of *a*-EPENTHESIS inserts the vowel *a* between the second and third of three consecutive consonants, creating two well-formed syllables where there had been one poorly-formed syllable. The rule of *i*-ADDITION inserts the vowel *i* at the end of a word ending in two contiguous consonants, performing the same ulterior function as *a*-EPENTHESIS. Less obvious is the fact that syllable structure constraints govern the morphological rules of FEMININE SUFFIX SELECTION in Akkadian: bases which end in a consonant cluster take the suffix *at* so that the second consonant attaches to the suffix-vowel and forms another syllable. The Akkadian rule of VOWEL DELETION respects the syllable structure constraints and fails to apply whenever it would produce a poorly-formed syllable.

Moreover, it will be argued below, in accord with some scholars, that Akkadian possessed a rule of VOWEL SHORTENING. This rule would delete a vowel segment, or shorten a long vowel, in a closed syllable. If this is so, we shall be able to establish two important generalizations about Akkadian syllable structure, aside from the well-known and common Semitic restrictions on consonant clusters. First, a syllable contains no more than three segments (with the possible exception of a word-final syllable having a long vowel). Second, in overweight syllables, i.e., those containing more than three segments, consonant clusters are resolved by adding a vocalic segment, thereby creating a new syllable; but double vowel segments, i.e., long vowels, in closed syllables are resolved by subtracting a vocalic segment. Thus in Akkadian well-formed syllables are produced through operations on vowels, not consonants.

In the sections that follow I shall establish, describe, and, when necessary, defend the above-mentioned rules (sections 3-7), as well as the apparent rules of syllabification in Akkadian (section 2). The relationships of these rules to syllable structure will be delineated in section 8.


## 1.3. The role of the syllable in phonology

No discourse on syllable structure can avoid the ironic fact that the syllable rarely plays a role in the grammars constructed by modern linguists. Despite the difficulty of the formal grammars in handling the syllable, a wide variety of studies have demonstrated the real importance of the syllable as a phonological unit (cf. Bell and Hooper 1978).

First, research in articulatory phonetics shows that speakers seem to organize minimal units of articulation into syllables (cf. MacNeilage and Ladefoged 1976:100-101). Although the syllable has eluded precise definition as a phonetic unit (Ladefoged 1971:81), it can still be acknowledged as a reality. This conclusion is corroborated on the acoustic side by findings that our auditory sense perceives incoming speech in syllabic units (Darwin 1976:199-201). Phonemes are articulated differently depending on their position in the syllable (Fujimura and Lovins 1978), and they are perceived according to the nuances effected by syllable-position (Lehiste 1970:49). The brain, therefore, must organize phonemes into syllables before it can command the motor organs of speech (cf. Lehiste 1970:155; Lisker 1978).

Inferential support for the psychological reality of the syllable may be adduced in a number of ways, most of which are summarized by Sommerstein (1977:199) and Kahn (1976:16-17). People have no trouble in dividing their speech into syllables and can count the number of syllables in a word or phrase (cf. Ladefoged 1971:81). Speakers who have a word on the tip of their tongue can often recall the number of syllables in that word. Aphasics and young children who cannot pronounce a word or phrase can often make articulatory gestures corresponding to the number of syllables in that word or phrase. Speech errors, such as spoonerisms, commonly involve syllables, and phonemes are often exchanged within the domain of the syllable (MacKay 1978).

More importantly for our study, a large number of phonological processes are most convincingly explained by reference to the domain of the syllable and syllabification. In Estonian, for instance, the duration of vowels in syllables other than the initial one depends directly on the number of the syllable's position in the word (Lehiste 1970:50-51). Reduplication and other processes of word-formation display sensitivity to the syllable (Bell and Hooper 1978; Ingram 1978; Lehiste 1978). Rules, such as one in Slovak (Kenstowicz and Kisseberth 1979:99-109), which disallow sequences of accented syllables, are surely syllable-sensitive.[1] In fact, suprasegmental, or prosodic, features such as stress, pitch, and tone often appear interdependent with syllabification (Lehiste 1970: 70, 82, 84, passim; cf. for stress, Liberman and Prince 1977; McCarthy 1979; Donegan and Stampe 1978; McCawley 1978; for tone, Wang 1964).

Phonological rules are increasingly being shown to operate at syllable-boundaries or within the circumscribed domain of the syllable. In Sanskrit "no syllable may both begin and end with a phonetically aspirated consonant" (Sommerstein 1977:58). Broselow (1979) has shown that in Cairene Arabic a pharyngealized consonant spreads its features of pharyngeality to all other segments within its own syllable. Lehiste (1970:46) demonstrates that Estonian "overlength," a higher degree of vowel length, devolves upon syllables rather than segments. Finally, as Kahn (1976:41-116) has persuasively argued for English, a number of phonological rules are conditioned by aspects of syllable structure (cf. Hooper 1972, 1976; Vennemann 1972a).

Considering the phonetic and phonological evidence for the psychological reality of the syllable and its functions in language, the present study is predicated upon the conviction that seeking the role which syllable structure plays in a number of rules of Akkadian phonology is more than a heuristic exercise; it is essential for the analysis of Akkadian.

## 1.4. Principles of phonological analysis

The linguistic study of Akkadian has by and large been a historical enterprise, and the vast majority of grammars and smaller researches have been guided by philological, rather than linguistic, concerns. The patent objective of the standard grammars and dialect studies has not been to describe the language but to provide the philologist with the means to interpret the various linguistic forms and syntactic constructions that will be encountered in Akkadian texts (cf. Speiser 1953:130a; Renger 1972:229). This is well and good. Problematic is the fact that most Akkadian grammars have explained synchronic processes in a historical, or diachronic, fashion (cf. Hirsch 1975:254). The most notable exception to the diachronic treatment of Akkadian is *A Linguistic Analysis of Akkadian* by Reiner (1966), which applied the developing generative theory of its day synchronically. Because Akkadian linguistics has, understandably, been so historically oriented, it is worthwhile to set forth the basic methodological principles employed in the present synchronic study.

I take the purpose of synchronic phonological analysis to be the identification and formulation of rules that would best derive actual phonetic realizations from their underlying, morphophonemic forms. For "language learning, like learning of any other kind, involves

---

[1]Cf. compensatory lengthening as a process of balancing adjacent syllables of different weights in Grundt (1976), Lehiste (1978), Donegan and Stampe (1978), Ingria (1980).

the induction of general rules from particular instances" (Fodor, Bever and Garrett 1974:
467-468). The procedure for accomplishing this task is as follows.[2] When the same morpheme is encountered in alternant phonetic, or surface, forms, I posit a single underlying
base form and seek out rules that will consistently and economically derive all alternating
surface forms from the same underlying base. For example, the imperative of the Akkadian
verb *šapaarum* 'to send' occurs as *šupur* for the masculine singular and *šuprii* for the
feminine singular. I would posit a single underlying form and a rule by which both surface forms could be derived (contrast Reiner 1966). If possible, I would attempt to posit
one of the allomorphic variants as the base form and derive the other allomorphs from the
one (cf. Kiparsky 1973:3-56; Vennemann 1974:346-348; Hooper 1976:111-138). In this
instance, we could derive *šuprii* from /šupur+ii/ by a rule that would delete the second
vowel; or we could derive *šupur* from /šupr/ by a rule that would insert the vowel *u*
between *p* and *r* (see further § 5.23 below).

When more than one analysis is available, as in the present example, we must have at our
disposal criteria for evaluating which analysis is preferable. Hyman (1975:91-98) has con-
veniently delineated the following five guidelines. First, the rules should derive all and only
correct phonetic realizations from the posited base forms. Second, simpler derivations are,
all things being equal, to be preferred. Third, the rule should conform "to the overall
pattern of the phonological system." Fourth, a derivation is favored if its individual com-
ponents - the phonemes, the morphemes, the phonological processes - can independently
be shown to exist in the language. And fifth, a rule is preferred if it describes a process
that is more "natural." (The term "natural" entails such considerations as: Is the process
observed in a variety of languages? Would a child tend to perform the process in trying
to articulate the forms (s)he hears? Would a speaker perform the process in rapid or
careless speech? Is the process common in phonological change?)

It must always be borne in mind that synchronic rules and underlying forms are by no
means to be equated automatically with diachronic changes and historically prior forms,
respectively. The synchronic order and form of the rules may be quite different from
historical counterparts (cf., e.g., Chafe 1970:37; King 1969:101-102; Kiparsky 1973:17-18).
Native speakers have only sparse and incidental knowledge of the history of their language. They induce the underlying forms and the rules from what they hear. These base
forms and rules may or may not be identical to historically reconstructed forms and rules.
Many synchronic rules and base forms do in fact reflect historical ancestors (cf. Saporta
1965; Greenberg 1979), but this may not be presupposed.

### 1.4.1. Synchronic reanalysis

The necessary dichotomy between historical and synchronic analysis is nowhere more
apparent than in the universal phenomenon of synchronic reanalysis. In this operation a
speaker's (synchronic) analysis of a current form diverges from the historical explanation
and produces novel forms. The phenomenon has been identified many times in Semitic,

---

[2]Here I follow most synoptic discussions of generative phonological theory, e.g., Harms (1968),
Schane (1973a), Hyman (1975), Sommerstein (1977), Kenstowicz and Kisseberth (1979). An ex-
cellent illustration is provided in the last-cited work, pp. 65-71.

both ancient and modern.[3]  A familiar example in Akkadian is the reanalysis of the I/3
(Gtn) form of the verb *'*iptarras* as /'iptan(a)ras/ (so Kuryłowicz 1972:25-26, 63; Renger
1972:230-232; Reiner 1966:95).[4]  At some preliterate time Akkadian speakers, possessing
a synchronic rule in which /n/ assimilates to a following consonant, secondarily analyzed
the double consonant in forms such as *'iptarras* not as geminate /rr/ but as /nr/. This,
then, led to the creation of forms with *n* occurring on the surface, such as *'iptanarras*,
the I/3 present form. Assuming this reconstruction is correct, historically the *n* was
morphophonemic and primary.[5]

## 1.5. Akkadian orthography

As a language that is no longer spoken, Akkadian cannot be subjected to acute phonetic
study (cf. Reiner 1966:20). Phonological phenomena involving allophonic variation, therefore, cannot be described with assurance. Nevertheless, since Akkadian was written for
the most part syllabically, with consonants and vowels, certain types of phonological
processes can be induced from the cuneiform orthography. Akkadian can be examined
phonologically in those areas in which systematic alternations indicate either regular
synchronic processes or diachronic changes or substitutions. Such phenomena include the
regular deletion, insertion, substitution, or assimilation of segments (cf. Greenstein 1980).

It is true that Akkadian orthography, like any scribal practice (cf. King 1969:204-206),
is often inconsistent, reflecting the influence of different writing systems (cf. Hirsch
1975:268; Greenstein and Marcus 1976:60-62). But it has been found that contrasting
spellings within the same dialect can generally be classified as either morphophonemic or
phonetic (Reiner 1966:56, 1973a, 1973b; Gelb 1970; Greenstein 1980). "Morphophonemic
writings represent the underlying structure of morphemes before they undergo phonological processes and are realized phonetically in speech. Phonetic writings approximate the
actual spoken form. Thus, for example, the word for 'sin' is written both *'arnu* and
*'annu* within the same dialect. . . *'arnu* is a morphophonemic spelling and. . . *'annu* is
phonetic, reflecting the assimilation of /rn/ to [nn]" (Greenstein 1980:52). By comparing
phonetic writings with underlying, morphophonemic ones, we can identify some phonological processes in Akkadian. Other processes, such as stress assignment (phonetic accentua-

---

[3]See, e.g., Poebel (1939:145) on the development of the Akkadian stative form *nanzuz*; Kuryłowicz
(1972:26) on the development of the liquid consonant as the second stem-consonant of quadriliteral verbs in Akkadian (cf. Reiner 1966:72-73); Hirsch (1975:307) on the development of
*'erbeneetu* as the plural of Akkadian *'erbettu*; Malone (1975:9) for the synchronic analysis of
Hebrew determination as *ha* + gemination of the following consonant; Johnstone (1975:21) for the
synchronic interpretation of the dual noun ending in Modern South Arabian, *i*, as the initial
segment in the word for 'two'.

[4]Contrast Poebel (1939:3, 41); von Soden (1969: § 20i); Gelb (1955:110a); Kienast (1957:46).
I concur with Lieberman (1977:84, n. 231) in positing a glottal stop preceding an otherwise
initial vowel in Akkadian.

[5] For the reanalysis of Akkadian *š* + pronominal *\*š* as /ss/ instead of the expected /šš/, see
Greenstein (1980); cf. also the reanalysis of [ss] in NA *'inašši* (etc.) as /ṣ/, explained in Parpola
(1974).  For specialized studies of reanalysis in languages other than Semitic, see, e.g., Andersen
(1973) and Haiman (1977).

tion), cannot be investigated with a high degree of confidence because they are not represented clearly in the orthography. On account of these limitations, a complete phonology of Akkadian can never be written.

## 1.6. Data

It is important for the phonological study of Akkadian to cull data from texts that can be assumed to best reproduce the spoken language. Literary texts in Akkadian tend to utilize archaic writing conventions (cf., e.g., Riemschneider 1976:71) and may entail non-colloquial, even artificial features.[6] This, together with the fact that less professional or stylized writing generally comes closer to representing the spoken language (cf. Anderson 1973:16), has led me to rely primarily on letters as a source of linguistic data (cf. Deller 1959; Aro 1955:38; Reiner 1966:22). Since the phenomena I investigate either occur in most dialects of Akkadian or require the establishment of historical and/or dialectal relationships, I have garnered evidence from dialects of diverse places and periods. A corpus of letters has been studied from each of the following dialects: Old Akkadian (OAkk.), Old Assyrian (OA), Old Babylonian (OB), Middle Babylonian (MB), and Neo-Assyrian (NA).[7] This corpus is often supplemented by royal and literary documents, as a control, and by data from other dialects and various specialized studies, especially for rarely instantiated forms and writings.

It is not necessary to include every text in every dialect in order to discern the predominant patterns (cf. Lévi-Strauss 1970:40). "In no field of inquiry is there such a thing as all the facts. There is no non-arbitrary cut-off to stop describing and begin explaining" (Anderson 1973:5; cf. Chomsky 1977:21). It is the object of the present study to explain certain facets of Akkadian phonology by regarding the trees insofar as they form a forest of a particular shape and texture. Another tree here or there will not alter our perception of the forest.

## 1.7. Sigla

It is the intention of this study to communicate with both linguists who have an interest in Akkadian phonology and/or syllable structure, and Assyriologists and other Semitists who are philologically inclined. For this reason I hope the reader will indulge a few explanations of the sigla herein employed.

Underlying representations are enclosed in slanted lines (/ /) and phonetic approximations in square brackets ([ ]). Transcriptions and orthographic representations are italicized. For reasons which will become clearer below, vowel length is indicated not by a

[6]Poebel (1939:101, 121), contrary to von Soden (1932-1933), contends that Akkadian poetry reflects colloquial language. This is no doubt true to some degree as in many respects all poetry must overlap with speech. My own studies, especially in §7.7 below, point up artificial features of Akkadian literary language.

[7]A precise list of the core corpus of texts is presented in Greenstein (1977:15).

macron but by a doubled vowel segment, e.g., long *a* is represented as *aa*. A word boundary is signified by #.

## 2. SYLLABIFICATION IN AKKADIAN

Before we can describe the Akkadian syllable, we must know its parameters. In an Akkadian string of the shape *CVVCVCCV*, for example, where are the syllable divisions? The present study assumes that the only correct syllabification for Akkadian is *CVV-CVC-CV*. This assumption can be supported by both general and internal considerations.

First, because the most basic syllable type universally is *CV*, a sequence of consonants and vowels should be syllabified, all things being equal, so as to maximize *CV* units (cf., e.g., Jakobson and Halle 1957:239-240; Hyman 1975:18-19; Sommerstein 1977:227; Bell and Hooper 1978:9).[8] Sequences of *CC* within syllables should not be assumed word-internally in Akkadian because Akkadian tolerates them neither in word-initial nor word-final position (cf. Kahn 1976). Moreover, a number of general theoretical studies conclude that a consonant flanked by vowels syllabifies with the following, not the preceding, vowel (e.g., Kahn 1976; Rudes 1977:14-15; Lowenstamm 1981). For the time being we shall leave the permissibility of a *CVVC* syllable in Akkadian an open question (see further § 6.0). Otherwise, we find that *CV*, *CVV*, and *CVC* are the only permissible syllable types in Akkadian.

Internal support for this position comes from the syllabic writing system of Akkadian (cf. esp. Gelb 1963:107-113).[9] Cuneiform signs represent either permissible syllable types (*CV*, *CVC*), fractions of syllables (*V*, *VC*), or two simple syllables (*CVCV*), but no impermissible syllables (such as any possessing a consonant cluster) or sequences overreaching syllable structure (such as *VCCV*; cf. Lieberman 1977:106, n. 308). In other words, the Akkadian writing system seems to be sensitive to implicit notions of the well-formed syllable.[10]

## 3. THE RULE OF *a*-EPENTHESIS

When a consonant-initial suffix is attached to a stem ending in a geminate consonant or to a stem followed immediately by the feminine suffix /t/, an underlying sequence of

---

[8]Schane et al. (1974/1975:352) summarize the lines of evidence that support this conclusion: 1) virtually all languages include this as one of their permissible syllable types; 2) *CVCV* patterns are the first emitted by young children; and 3) in many languages various rules transform more complex strings into *CVCV* patterns.

[9] For the notion that writing systems often support the reality of the syllable, cf. Sommerstein (1977:199).

[10]For a study in which cuneiform writing is shown to be sensitive to underlying phonemic values, see Greenstein (1980). Lieberman (1977:551-558) adduces neurological evidence to support an intrinsic nexus between syllable graphemes and linguistic competence.

three consonants develops. All Akkadian dialects break up the cluster by inserting the vowel *a* between the second and third consonants. Examples are:

| | |
|---|---|
| /tupp+šu/ | 'his tablet' (AbB 6 #72:13) |
| [tuppašu] | *a*-EPENTHESIS |
| /'umm+ša/ | 'her mother' (YOS 13 #192:7) |
| ['ummaša] | *a*-EPENTHESIS |
| /maqit+t+šu/ | 'its ruins' (JAOS 70, 70:34) |
| [maqittašu] | *a*-EPENTHESIS |

That the epenthetic vowel is short, and in all probability unstressed, is demonstrable in Assyrian dialects in which this vowel undergoes VOWEL HARMONY, assimilating to the vowel in the following syllable.[11] Compare the following examples in OA:

| | |
|---|---|
| [tuppaka] | 'your tablet' (Kienast ATHE #28:25) |
| [tuppini] | 'our tablet' (ibid.:22) |
| [tuppušu] | 'his tablet' (ibid.:28) |

We may formulate the rule provisionally as follows:

Insert the vowel /a/ in the environment /CC_C/.

This process creates a new syllable and eliminates all consonant clusters.


## 4. THE RULE OF *i*-ADDITION

When a word ends in two underlying consonants, all Akkadian dialects break up the cluster and create another syllable by attaching the vowel /i/ (or /ə/, see below) to the end of the cluster. Such a cluster may emerge in two ways, analogous to the contexts that occasion *a*-EPENTHESIS.

One context is that of the bound (construct) form of noun bases ending in a geminate consonant, such as /libb/ 'heart of' → [libbi]. It should be noted that a subset of geminate bases form their bound forms by dropping the second member of the geminate pair. Well-known examples are [šar] from /šarr/ 'king' and [kunuk] from /kunukk/ 'seal' (cf. von Soden 1969:§64e). This constitutes the single exception to the generaliza-

---

[11]For OA, cf. Hirsch (1967:324; 1972:411; 1975:281, n. 114), Kienast (1960:41); for MA, e.g. *melammušu* 'his aura' (AKA 33:41), cf. Mayer (1971:§13-3); for NA, e.g., *dullušu* 'his work' (AOS 6, #53: obv. 12), *madaktušu* 'his killing' (ibid., #11: rev. 14); for OB Mari, e.g., *rummukunu* (ARM I, 19:7).

tion that Akkadian resolves consonant clusters through operations on vowels only (see § 1.2 above and § 8.6 below). However, the distinction between bases that use *i*-ADDI-TION and those that use what we may call GEMINATE CONSONANT TRUNCATION is conditioned not phonologically but lexically. This may be confirmed by the fact that, especially in OA and OB, the same stem may form its bound form either way. Compare OA [šarra] (apparently [šarrə]) beside [šar] 'king', OB [kakki] beside [kak] 'weapon' (von Soden 1969:§ 64e), and OB [lib] (VAB 6 # 134:15) beside [libbi].

The second context in which *i*-ADDITION applies is in the bound forms of feminine nouns that take the suffix /t/, such as [napišti] and [tukulti].

Despite the fact that the vowel that is added is nearly always written *i*, many scholars interpret the vowel phonetically as schwa, [ə] (e.g., von Soden 1969:§§8d, 64e; Goetze 1946:191, n. 25, 194; Diakonoff 1965:60, n. 17; Mayer 1971:§13-2). This interpretation has been challenged (Gelb 1955:98b; Hirsch 1975:270), particularly on the grounds that the vowel is consistently written *i*. This is not entirely true of OB, however, where in addition to *libbi*, for example, one finds — albeit less frequently — *libba* (Lipit-Ištar Cone 18) and *libbu* (AbB 1, 2:10; VAB 6 ##218:22. 260:14; et al.).[12] This orthographic variation appears to reflect a stage at which the employment of *i* had not yet become fully standardized. Most probably the orthographic convention was devised to render a neutral, minimal "Murmelvokal." The *i*, then, may be regarded as an orthographic representation of phonetic [ə]. The selection of *i* to render schwa finds phonetic support in that schwa is often characterized as a mid front vowel (Hooper 1976:235-236). Moreover, the use of *i* as an epenthetic-like vowel has parallels in other branches of Semitic (Bravmann 1977 [1938]:3-93); cf., e.g., the usage of the aleph-*i* sign to represent vowelless aleph in Ugaritic (Fronzaroli 1955:38-41). This schwa sufformative clearly functions to create a minimal syllable with the second word-final consonant.[13] We may formulate the rule for the present as follows:

Insert the vowel *i* in the environment CC_#.

## 5. THE RULE OF VOWEL DELETION

### 5.1. Initial formulation

Nearly all grammatical descriptions of Akkadian have included a rule of VOWEL DELETION, which we may formulate as follows:

[12] Alternatively, it is possible, as Prof. W. L. Moran has pointed out to me, that these cases of *libbu* reflect an archaic locative *u(m)* suffix with a pleonastic preposition since each is preceded by a preposition. At Mari there is a *takitta* for *takitti* (ARM II, 26:11), but it may represent a sandhi phenomenon as the next word begins with *'a* (cf. Finet 1956:§7c).

[13] Jensen (1978:672) does well to emphasize that the definition of minimal vowels is language-specific and, contra Hooper (1976), that languages do not necessarily deploy the minimal vowel for epenthesis. Akkadian, as we have seen, employs *a*, not *i*, for epenthesis.

Delete a short vowel in the environment VC_CV.

There are a number of restrictions on the rule in various dialects, and these will be discussed below. We shall also take up the oft-proposed suggestion that stress needs be incorporated into the rule.

The chief evidence for Akkadian VOWEL DELETION are the systematic alternations between forms such as the 3 masc. sg. stative verb-form and the 3 fem. sg. stative, e.g.:

*damiq*    'he is good'    *lemun*    'he is bad'    *rapaš*    'he is wide'

*damqat*    'she is good'    *lemnet*    'she is bad'    *rapšat*    'she is wide'

Following our principles in § 1.4 above, we should posit the masculine forms as the underlying bases and derive the feminine forms by means of VOWEL DELETION:

| UNDERLYING | /damiq+at/ | /lemun+at/ | /rapaš+at/ |
|---|---|---|---|
| VOWEL DELETION | [damqat] | [lemnet][14] | [rapšat] |

Although the evidence for Akkadian VOWEL DELETION looks straightforward, the synchronic existence of the rule has been seriously questioned. With respect to a rule of VOWEL DELETION Reiner (1966:118) has this to say: "We may use it with profit because it requires a single rule for deleting the vowel regardless of its quality. Its disadvantages are that such a rule does not seem to be needed for the description of other aspects of the morphology." Accordingly, Reiner posits two morphemes, say, /damiq/ and /damq/, to account for the alternations. I shall proceed to demonstrate that the principle of positing a unitary base and deriving alloforms phonologically should be sustained and that VOWEL DELETION must be implemented in the analysis of a number of systematic alternations in Akkadian.


## 5.2. Evidence for VOWEL DELETION

### 5.2.1. Stative/adjective alternations

The stative form of the verb, a predicate that is generally intransitive (Buccellati 1968),[15] and the adjective that is derived from the stative as its base (e.g., Ungnad 1903:369; Bravmann 1977 [1947]:181; Castellino 1962:91ff.; Kuryłowicz 1972:65 et passim)[16] display regular patterns in which forms of the shape *CVCVC* (cases a and e) alternate with forms of the shape *CVCC* . . . (cases b, c, d):

---

[14] The vowel *e* both in the base and the suffix is historically derived from *a* (cf. von Soden 1969: § 9b).

[15] For transitive uses of the stative, see Rowton (1962).

[16] For classifying verbs and adjectives within a single lexical category universally, see Lakoff (1970:10-11, 115-133) and J. McCawley's remarks in the forward to ibid., vi, n. 3.

| (1a) | *damiq* | 'he is good' |
| (1b) | *damqu* | 'he is good' (subjunctive) |
| (1c) | *damqat* | 'she is good' |
| (1d) | *damqu(m)* | 'good' (masc. sg.) |
| (1e) | *damiqtu(m)* | 'good' (fem. sg.) |
| | | |
| (2a) | *lemun* | 'he is bad' |
| (2b) | *lemnu* | 'he is bad' (subjunctive) |
| (2c) | *lemnet* | 'she is bad' |
| (2d) | *lemnu(m)* | 'bad' (masc. sg.) |
| (2e) | *lemuttu(m)*[17] | 'bad' (fem. sg.) |
| | | |
| (3a) | *rapaš* | 'he is wide' |
| (3b) | *rapšu* | 'he is wide' (subjunctive) |
| (3c) | *rapšat* | 'she is wide' |
| (3d) | *rapšu(m)* | 'wide' (masc. sg.) |
| (3e) | *rapaštu(m)* | 'wide' (fem. sg.) |

Historically, most scholars would derive both the stative and the adjectival formations from a predicative state of the noun (e.g., Goetze 1942; Haldar 1963:260-261; Castellino 1962:39, 42ff.; Buccellati 1968; Kuryłowicz 1972:93, 95 et passim; Hodge 1975; Janssens 1975). While most Semitists take the base form of primary nouns to be of the shape /CVCC/ both historically and synchronically (see below), they generally take the base form of predicate derivations, historically and synchronically, to be /CVCVC/ (e.g., Poebel 1939:70 with n. 1; von Soden 1969:§§55e-g; Goetze 1946b; Aro 1965: 407).

In terms of the Semitic patterning of vowel schemes interdigitated across a consonantal root (e.g., Goshen-Gottstein 1964; Cohen 1970:31-48; Malone 1979/1980), the underlying base of the stative/adjective is usually a /C-C-C/ root with a /-V-V-/ scheme. The motivation for positing this base form is obvious. The first vowel, *a* (or the historically secondary *e*), always appears, and the second vowel, *i, u,* or *a* (in descending order of frequency), is consistent but unpredictable by phonological rule. Therefore, we must posit an underlying second vowel in the base form (contra Reiner 1966:53; Edzard 1973:136-138) and extract three vowel schemes: /a − i/, /a − u/, and /a − a/.[18]   Cases b, c, d in which the second schematic vowel does not appear, are derived by the VOWEL DELETION rule (cf., e.g., von Soden 1969:§§12b, c; Ungnad and Matouš 1969:§63f).

---

[17] The underlying form is /lemun+t+u(m)/; the /n/ assimilates to the following /t/ according to rule.

[18] It happens that the same root may occur with different schemes in different dialects as a result of phonological change; cf., e.g., *wašab* in OA (e.g., CCT I, 44:10) but *wašib* in OB (e.g., PBS I/2, 7:6).

### 5.2.2. Unbound/bound alternations in feminine noun forms

Certain feminine nouns exhibit alternations between their unbound and bound/construct forms, such as:

| *Unbound* | *Bound/Construct* | |
|-----------|-------------------|---|
| 'amtu    | 'amat             | 'bondwoman' |
| biltu    | bilat             | 'tribute' |
| šattu    | šanat             | 'year' |

As I shall demonstrate at length in § 7 below, we must posit underlying /'amat/, /bilat/, and /šanat/. When vocalic suffixes are attached, VOWEL DELETION produces, e.g., ['amtu], [biltu], and [šattu] (with the rule of /nC/ assimilation), which are the correct forms.

### 5.2.3. G-stem imperative alternations

The case of the G-stem imperative is more complicated. The suffixless form, viz., the masculine singular, appears in the shape *CVCVC* while the suffix-bearing forms have no vowel between the second and third stem-consonants. Note the following examples:

|     | *2 masc. sg.* | *2 masc. pl.* | |
|-----|---------------|---------------|---|
| (a) | šukun         | šuknaa        | 'set' |
| (b) | ṣabat         | ṣabtaa        | 'seize' |
| (c) | piqid         | piqdaa        | 'charge' |
| (d) | 'alik         | 'alkaa        | 'go' |
| (e) | 'amur         | 'amraa        | 'see' |
| (f) | bini[19]      | binaa         | 'build' |
| (g) | 'uṣur         | 'uṣraa        | 'guard' |
| (h) | 'idin         | 'innaa[20]    | 'give' |
| (i) | limad         | limdaa        | 'know' |
| (j) | tišab         | tišbaa        | 'dwell' |

Most verbs form their G-stem imperatives according to the patterns exemplified in cases (a, b, c), in which the two vowels are identical. Moreover, in all of the cases the second vowel also appears in the preterite form of the verbs in question; e.g., *'iškun, 'iṣbat, 'illik, 'iimur,* etc. Taking these two facts into consideration, many grammars of Akkadian posit only the second vowel of the imperative on the underlying level. The first vowel

---

[19] For OA *kila, taru*, see Ungnad and Matouš (1969: § 83e).

[20] From underlying /'idinaa/, with VOWEL DELETION (producing 'idnaa) and HOMORGANIC CONSONANT ASSIMILATION (producing ['innaa]). For the latter rule, see now Greenstein (1980: 55-56 with n. 35, 62).

they derive *via* a rule of epenthesis that inserts a copy of the putative stem-vowel between the first and second consonants (e.g., Poebel 1939:99-100, n. 1; von Soden 1969: § 18b; Ungnad and Matouš 1969: § § 11a, 63e; Edzard 1973:125 et passim; Blau 1977:30).

This analysis is, however, fundamentally diachronic, not synchronic, and may be incorrect in any event. It reconstructs the second vowel of the imperative and the stem-vowel of the preterite from a verbal root that is characterized by this vowel (e.g., von Soden 1969: § § 50c, 73c; Speiser 1953:135a; Castellino 1962:43, 45, 53; Diakonoff 1965:29, 33, 35; Kuryłowicz 1972:34-35, 43-44). Some studies derive the imperative from the preterite (e.g., Martin 1957; Sekine 1973:216), and some derive the preterite from the imperative (e.g., Poebel 1939:133; Dahood, Deller and Köbert 1965:38). Even from a diachronic standpoint this analysis of the imperative is difficult. Although it can account for cases (a-h), it cannot account for cases such as (i, j) (cf. Gelb 1955:110a). One could explain the first vowel in cases (a-h) by a diachronic process of epenthesis and ablaut, but one cannot explain the vowel *i* in cases such as (i, j) by recourse to vowel-copy. For these and other reasons, some scholars reconstruct an imperative of disyllabic shape (e.g., Poebel 1939:99-100, n. 1, 135; Gelb 1969; Dahood, Deller and Köbert 1965:42).

One could explain cases (a-h) by appeal to an ablaut process affecting an already existent vowel. Cases such as (i, j) would then represent exceptions to the ablaut. Support for this reconstruction can be adduced from Old Akkadian and Old Assyrian, in which the hypothesized ablaut process has affected some stems which in Babylonian preserve the /i − a/ scheme; compare OA *tašab* with OB *tišab* (references in Hecker 1968a:162; for OAkk., von Soden 1969: § 87e). Moreover, cases (d, e) are also exceptional and may be explained as follows. An initial laryngeal either influenced a vowel other than *a* to change to *a* or prevented an original *a* from undergoing ablaut. To sum up, an imperative formation with a two-vowel scheme can be plausibly reconstructed.

Synchronically, a two-vowel scheme must be posited. Since the vowel between the first and second consonants is present in every allomorph, it must be posited underlyingly (see § 1.4 above and cf. Reiner 1966:76). Were there no underlying vowel following the first consonant, it would be difficult to derive cases (g, h). The first vowel could not be motivated - unless one were to posit an underlying initial /n/, which can be reconstructed historically perhaps but is difficult to motivate synchronically. [21]  The genuine problem is to determine whether the suffix-bearing forms (*šuknii*, *šuknaa*, *šuknam*, etc.) are to be derived from an underlying base identical to that of the suffixless form (e.g., *šukun*) or whether the suffixless form is to be derived from a one-vowel base through a rule of vowel-copy insertion (e.g., /šukn/ → [šukun]).

Reiner (1966:77) opts for the latter solution. In this way the derivation of the suffixless imperative resembles the derivation of the bound/construct forms of *CVCC*-shaped (segolate) nouns (see § § 5.24-5.2424 below). However, as Reiner herself concedes, such a solution cannot derive cases such as (d, e, i, j). Rather, we should posit for the imperative underlying schemes of two vowels: /u − u/ (or /a,e − u/ for initial-weak stems), /i − i/

---

[21] There is, in fact, diachronic evidence that militates against positing initial /n/. In OA the imperative form *'idin* 'give' became *din* (e.g., TCL 20, 111:24); cf. plural *dinaa* (ibid.: 8, 19).

(or /a,e — i/ for initial-weak stems), /a — a/, or /i — a/. Every stem would then be marked in the lexicon for the appropriate scheme. The alternant forms in which no vowel appears between the second and third stem-consonants can be derived unexceptionally by VOWEL DELETION (cf., e.g., Ungnad and Matouš 1969: § 63e; Kuryłowicz 1972:45).

This analysis is supported by the existence of morphophonemic spellings (see § 1.5 above) of a two-vowel G-stem imperative with suffixes in OA; contrast *šu-ku-nam* 'deposit for me' (TCL 19, 1:29) beside *šu-uk-nam* (ibid.:22).[22] In the former case the base form /šukun+am/ is written without regard to VOWEL DELETION while in the latter case the fully derived from, [šuknam], is written. The most straightforward and exceptionless analysis of the imperative alternations, therefore, posits underlying stems of the shape /CVCVC/ and implements VOWEL DELETION to produce allomorphic variants. The process that assigns the vowels is not phonological but morphological.

### 5.2.4.   Unbound/bound alternations on /CVCVC/ masculine nouns

Masculine nouns with bases of the shape /CVCVC/ display an allomorphy between bound/ construct forms and the unbound, suffix-bearing forms which is best explained by reference to VOWEL DELETION. The majority of such nouns have identical vowels in the two syllables, the first of which is lexical:

| *Bound/construct* | *Unbound* | |
|---|---|---|
| pagar | pagru(m) | 'corpse' |
| rigim | rigmu(m) | 'voice' |
| zumur | zumru(m) | 'body' |

Theoretically the second vowel could be produced by a phonological rule of vowel-copy insertion, which, as we shall see, is the way that most Akkadian grammarians explain it. There are, however, a respectable number of nouns which have schemes of two different vowels, e.g.:

| *Bound/construct* | *Unbound* | |
|---|---|---|
| šakin | šaknu(m) | 'official' |
| wakil | waklu(m) | 'overseer'[23] |
| 'apil | 'aplu(m) | 'son/heir' |
| qerub | qerbu(m) | 'midst'[24] |

In these examples the second vowel cannot be predicted by phonological rule and must, therefore, be underlying. Since there is no independent reason to segregate these two sets

---

[22] For other examples, see Gelb (1955:101b), Hirsch (1971:400, 419-420). For *i-di-na* beside *id-na* in Nuzi Akkadian, see Jucquois (1966:185).

[23] See Goetze (1947a:73, n. 3) for OB examples.

[24] For *qereb*; see Goetze (1948:86).

of examples, the bound/construct forms should be posited underlyingly and the unbound, suffix-bearing forms derived by VOWEL DELETION (cf., e.g., Ungnad and Matouš 1969: § 41f).

### 5.2.4.1.  CHALLENGES BY APPEAL TO EPENTHESIS AND PUTATIVE VOWEL COPY

Most grammars of Akkadian derive the bound/construct forms of putative /pagr/, /rigm/, /zumr/, etc., through a rule of epenthesis in which a copy of the stem-vowel is inserted between the second and third consonants, yielding [pagar], [rigim], [zumur], etc. (e.g., von Soden 1969: § 18a; Reiner 1966:52 et passim; Ungnad and Matouš 1969: § § lla, 41e). This proposed synchronic process reflects the historical development reconstructed by many Semitists (e.g., Speiser 1967:374, 390-391; Moscati 1969: § 9.17; Diakonoff 1965: 60; O'Leary 1969:134). A notable group of Semitists reconstructs the original shape of these nouns with a two-vowel scheme (e.g., Eilers 1935:16*; Dahood, Deller and Köbert 1965:42; Gelb 1969:13 et passim; Kuryłowicz 1972:135 et passim). The historical problem is a knotty one, particularly when one acknowledges that a single original stem may have been developed in different formations in different Semitic languages (cf., e.g., Bravmann 1977 [1938]:17-19; Steiner 1975).

Reiner (1966:52) formulates two rules of epenthesis synchronically. One inserts a copy vowel between two consonants at the beginning of a word (cf. von Soden 1969: § 18b; Ungnad and Matouš 1969: § 11a). This rule is meant to account for alternations in the G-stem imperative paradigm, discussed in § 5.23 above.[25] Such a proposal is unconvincing because it derives by phonological rule the only vowel in the paradigm that is immutable. Reiner's second rule inserts a (not always copy) vowel between two consonants at the end of a word (cf. von Soden 1969: § 18a; Ungnad and Matouš 1969: § 11a). This rule is intended to account for the second vowel in the bound/construct forms of masculine nouns such as *pagar, rigim,* and *zumur,* as well as other forms.[26] There are a number of difficulties with this proposal, of both a substantive and formal nature.

One substantive problem is that the same synchronic process that is alleged to insert a copy vowel between the second and third stem-consonants of /pagr/, /rigm/, and /zumr/ would also allegedly insert the second vowel in the feminine nouns *šalamtu* 'corpse', *šipirtu* 'message', *puluḫtu* 'fear', etc. (cf., e.g., Ungnad and Matouš 1969: § 37e). This, however, cannot be the case. As we shall see in § 7 below, Akkadian possessed two feminine suffix morphs, /t/ for stems of the shape /CVCVC/ and /at/ᵗ for stems of the shape /CVCC/. Were the underlying bases of *šalamtu, šipirtu,* and *puluḫtu* /šalm/, /šipr/, and /pulḫ/, respectively, they would each take the suffix /at/, yielding incorrect *\*šalmatu, \*šipretu,* and *\*pulḫatu.* The synchronic rules of FEMININE SUFFIX SELECTION indicate /šalam/, /šipir/, and /puluḫ/ underlyingly. The two-vowel scheme of identical vowels is therefore a morphological pattern and not phonologically determined. Contrast feminine

---

[25] Reiner (1966:78) also uses it to derive the first *a*-vowel in the present form of the G-stem verb, *'iparras,* but this vowel is more plausibly morphological, not phonological.

[26] Among these other forms are the fem. sg. adjective *damiqtu,* which Reiner (1966:78) derives from /damq+t+u/, and the 3 fem. sg. stative *parsat,* which she derives from /pars+t/. According to our methodology ( § 1.4) both of these derivations are unacceptable. In the first case the vowel *i* is phonologically unpredictable and in the second the vowel *a* is invariant and, consequently, morphophonemic. The underlying feminine suffix on the stative is unexceptionally /at/, not /t/.

nouns such as *kalbatu* 'bitch' that select the suffix /at/. Such nouns must be derived from monosyllabic morphemes such as /kalb/.

We may find additional support for positing underlying /CVCVC/ bases for feminine nouns such as *šalamtu, šipirtu,* and *puluḫtu* in the plurals of nouns of this type having /r/ as the third stem-consonant. Because, as we shall see in § § 5.511-5.512, VOWEL DELETION often fails to apply to vowels preceding /r/, underlying patterns of two vowels are preserved in the surface forms of such nouns, e.g.:

| *singular* | *plural* | |
| --- | --- | --- |
| nukurtu | nukuraatu | 'hostilities' |
| puzurtu | puzuraatu | 'secret places' |
| šipirtu | šipireetu | 'messages' |
| 'uṣurtu | 'uṣuraatu | 'designs' |

This phenomenon has been most commonly regarded as a secondary diachronic development in which the second vowel is inserted on account of the syllabicity of /r/ (e.g., Speiser 1967:387; von Soden 1969:§18c; Moscati 1969:§9.17). In later dialects, such as Neo-Assyrian, such a diachronic change did transpire. In early and literary Akkadian, however, instances of vowel-retention preceding /r/ represent an underlying two–vowel scheme (cf. Gelb 1955:100b; 1961:126-127); e.g., *ú-ṣú-ra-tim, ú-ṣú-ra-tu-ú-a* (CH prolog 3:31; epilog 24:91; literary OB); *nu-kúr-a-tum* (Reiner and Pingree 1975:55, #48; cf. 51, #39; OB); *pu-zu-ra-tú* (En. el. IV:132, variant in Gurney 1954-1956:354; SB). The later diachronic development in NA inserted a vowel where an earlier process of syncope had deleted that vowel.

As in the case of the G-stem imperative (§5.23 above), most of the synchronic morphological patterns comprised sets of identical vowels. But again like the G-stem imperative, there are also schemes of two different vowels in feminine nouns with disyllabic bases, such as *napištu, maqittu,* and *lemuttu.* The putative copy vowel in *šalamtu, šipirtu,* and *puluḫtu* similarly results not from a phonological process but from morphological patterning. The same appears to apply in the case of the second vowel in the masculine nouns *pagar, rigim, zumur,* etc.[27]

Another difficulty that besets the epenthesis theory of accounting for the second vowel in *pagar, rigim,* and *zumur* is posed by the so-called status indeterminatus. This is a predicate state in which a noun appears without case-endings, e.g., *'awiilum šuu šarraaq* "that man is a thief" (CH§7:55-56). Contrary to the assertions of some scholars (e.g., Ravn 1949:301; Buccellati 1968; von Soden 1969:§62c; Ungnad and Matouš 1969:§54), the status indeterminatus is not equivalent to a noun inflected as a stative (cf. Reiner 1970:

---

[27] One is tempted to adduce further support from a possible case of morphophonemic spelling of *šulmiika* 'your well-being' (gen.) in OB, viz., *šu-lum-mi-ka* AbB 1, 21:10). It is more likely, however, that this writing is a scribal error for *šu-ul-mi-ka,* contaminated by the word *šu-lum-ka* in the following line; cf. the note by F. R. Kraus, loc. cit.

292; Hirsch 1975:308). The distinction may be upheld in the feminine plural where one finds stativized predicates of the type *sinnišaa* 'they are women', *'almanaa* 'They are widows' (Hirsch 1975:311) but no status indeterminatus of the type *\*sinnišaat* 'are women' (cf. Castellino 1962:92). One also encounters a differentiation between *ḫaliq* 'it is lost' (stative) and *ḫalaq* 'it is a lost object' (status indeterminatus) (cf. Moscati 1969:§16.2). The status indeterminatus also serves as a form of the vocative (cf. Kraus 1976). Phonetic spellings are hard to come by as vocatives are frequently not in status indeterminatus and as they are usually written logographically. But some phonetically written examples are: *'etel* 'O man!' (Gilg., p. 22, iv:18), *barbar* 'O Wolf!' (BWL 194:13), *[k]alab* 'O dog!' (BWL 196:19), *taliim* 'O brother!' (BWL 218:51), *šamaš* 'O Sun!' (BWL 218:14), *kikkiš* 'O fence!' (Gilg. XI:21), *'igaar* 'O wall!' (loc. cit.).[28]

The simplest synchronic analysis is to explain the status indeterminatus as the underlying form of the noun minus case-endings (so Gelb 1969:5). Hearing both the unbound form of the noun, with case endings, and the status indeterminatus form, the Akkadian speaker could induce the underlying form of [kalbu] 'dog' as /kalab+u/, just as (s)he would induce the underlying form of [barbaru] 'wolf' as /barbar+u/. Since the bound/construct forms of the noun are formally equivalent to the status indeterminatus, it seems preferable to posit an underlying scheme of two vowels in the bound/construct forms, too, and derive the unbound forms through the VOWEL DELETION rule.

It is still possible to deny this unitary explanation of the status indeterminatus and argue that the underlying form of *kalab* 'O dog!' is /kalb/ (minus the case-ending) and that the second *a* is inserted phonologically. Such a position, however, not only requires a two-fold interpretation of the status indeterminatus, it also requires a rule of vowel-copy insertion that would often function redundantly. In many instances the forms to which putative vowel copy applies meet the structural descriptions of *a*-EPENTHESIS (§3) and *i*-ADDITION (§4), which are independently motivated. If [kalab] were derived from /kalb/ phonologically, why shouldn't *i*-ADDITION apply — as it does to /libb/ and /tukul+t/ — and produce (incorrect) *[kalbi]? (See further Greenstein 1977:36-37.)

5.2.4.2. SOME /CVCVC/ BOUND FORMS ARE PRODUCED MORPHOLOGICALLY

Rather, the second *a* in *kalab* is produced synchronically by morphological patterning, which interdigitates a /-a-a-/ scheme across a triconsonantal root. This becomes clear when we compare certain masculine nouns of /CVCVC/ shape in their bound/construct forms with their feminine counterparts. Feminine nouns such as *šalamtu, šipirtu,* and *puluḫtu* have underlying stems possessing two vowels and take the feminine suffix /t/ (see above §5.22 and esp. §7 below). Feminine nouns such as *'ardatu* 'slave' and *kalbatu* 'bitch', however, take the suffix /at/ and have underlying stems possessing only one vowel, viz., /'ard/ and /kalb/. To be consistent, we should posit the same monosyllabic bases for the respective masculine nouns *'ardu* ( < *wardum*) 'slave' and *kalbu* 'dog'. Consequently, the status indeterminatus and bound/construct form of such underlyingly monosyllabic nouns must be derived by morphological schematization.

---

[28] The identification of a vocative *šar* 'O king!' (von Soden 1950:155) was mistaken; see Held (1961:20a) on IV:14.

The source of this synchronic patterning may indeed have been a diachronic process of epenthesis. Consider such nouns as *pagru(m)*, *rigmu(m)*, and *zumru(m)*. When case-endings were preserved in the construct form (data and discussion in von Soden 1932:208ff.), the underlying consonant cluster in /pagr/, /rigm/, and /zumr/ was resolved by the vowel of the case-ending. But when case-endings were dropped in the construct, the underlying cluster was resolved by diachronic processes, including the epenthesis of a copy vowel. This early change is paralleled in Neo- and Late Babylonian when case-endings were dropped altogether. Word-final consonant clusters were then broken up by means of epenthesis, as native writings and foreign transcriptions testify (Ungnad 1923:425-426; Rimalt 1933/1934:124b). However, since all construct and bound forms displayed a second vowel on the surface, since the disyllabic status indeterminatus bore a superficial resemblance to it, and since nouns with two original vowels formed constructs with two different vowels, it seems likely that the two-vowel scheme became morphologized and was posited synchronically as underlying. To put it slightly differently, the originally epenthetic vowel was reanalyzed (see § 1.41 above) as the second vowel of a morphological scheme. An analogous case of reinterpreting an epenthetic vowel in Mohawk, an Amerindian language, is presented in Kiparsky (1973a:72-75).

The morphological status of the two-vowel scheme is empirically corroborated by formations such as the adverb *'ašariš* 'in the place' from underlying /'ašar+iš/. The second /a/ is constrained from deleting by the following /r/ (see § 5.511 below). Were the second /a/ analyzed by speakers as phonologically inserted, the adverb would have been realized as *\*ašriš* from *\*/'ašr+iš/*. In fact, the sufformative /iš/ must be attached to a two-vowel base, viz., /'ašar/. The form *'ašriš* emerges only in later periods when the constraint on the elision of *a* before /r/ is relaxed.

### 5.2.4.3. A HYPOTHETICAL OBJECTION FROM ASSYRIAN

Objections to my morphological analysis of bound/construct forms such as *kalab* (§ 5.242) might be raised on the basis of Assyrian evidence. In Assyrian the putative epenthetic vowel is often not a copy of the preceding vowel but rather *a*, as in *rigam* for Babylonian *rigim*, *rikas* for Bab. *rikis*, *šipar* for Bab. *šipir*, and *'uzan* for Bab. *'uzun* (cf. von Soden 1969:§ 18a; Hecker 1968b:§ 63h; Mayer 1971:§ 13-1). This phenomenon, however, reflects a phonological change in Assyrian in which an unstressed short vowel often became *a*. See n. 18 above for the correspondence of OA *wašab* : OB *wašib* in the stative and § 5.23 above for OA *tašab* : OB *tišab* in the G-stem imperative. This diachronic change finds a parallel in Sumerian in which a process of ablaut swept over disyllabic morphemes and left in its wake such forms as *amar*, *lipiš*, and *umun* (Gragg 1973:41).

### 5.2.5. Verb form alternations

VOWEL DELETION also operates in the derivation of various verbal forms, a function which has been widely recognized since Poebel (1939). Compare, e.g., the participle of the N-conjugation, *mupparsu(m)*, with its construct *mupparis* and the preterite *'ipparis* (e.g., Poebel 1939:35, 107; Goetze 1947b:51; von Soden 1969:12\*-13\*; Ungnad and Matouš 1969:§ § 62b, 66b, 67c). Since the vowel *i* in *paris* cannot be introduced by an independently motivated rule of epenthesis, it must be morphophonemic and part of the morphological paradigm. The participle bearing case-endings, *mupparsu(m)*, derives from the application of VOWEL DELETION to underlying /mu+n(a)+paris+u/. Analogous examples have been identified in the paradigms of other derived conjugations.

### 5.2.6. Primae-*w* G-stem preterite alternations

When the so-called ventive suffix is appended to the G-stem preterite of initial-\**w* verbs, VOWEL DELETION produces the resultant forms. Consider such alternations as *'ubil* 'he brought' (e.g., MAD 1, 169, ii:11; OAkk.) but *'ublam* 'he brought here' (e.g., MAD 5, 80:6; OAkk.); *'urid* 'he came down' (e.g., AbB 1, 27:14; OB). Again, since the vowel *i* is morphophonemic, the suffixed forms require VOWEL DELETION. [29]

### 5.2.7. Summary of VOWEL DELETION contexts

Synchronic analysis has identified allomorphic alternations in the following Akkadian paradigms: (1) the stative/adjective, (2) monosyllabic feminine nouns selecting the suffix /at/, (3) the G-stem imperative, (4) disyllabic noun stems, (5) derived conjugations of the verb, and (6) the G-stem of certain initial-*w* verbs. In each context one or more of the allomorphs is most straightforwardly explained by means of the VOWEL DELETION rule. Having established the rule itself, our next task is to formulate a precise yet non-redundant description of VOWEL DELETION in the various Akkadian dialects.

### 5.3. Diachronic vs. synchronic aspects of VOWEL DELETION

Before VOWEL DELETION became a synchronic rule of Akkadian it had left its mark diachronically. The synchronic rule differs from the historical change (cf. § 1.4 above). A synchronic description of VOWEL DELETION must be chary of including diachronic features that are not germane to the rule. For example, early grammars of Akkadian, such as Delitzsch (1906: § § 45a,b), describe a process of vowel syncopation in the context /VVC_/, which may have occurred historically but does not accord with the synchronic rule.

### 5.4. VOWEL DELETION does not depend upon STRESS

We have formulated VOWEL DELETION provisionally more or less as Goetze had (1946b, 1947c):

> Delete a vowel in the environment VC_CV.

Nearly all other descriptions of Akkadian VOWEL DELETION, including those published after Goetze's classic studies, introduce STRESS into the context of the rule (e.g., Ryckmans 1938: § 27; Poebel 1939:48; Ungnad and Matouš 1969: § 7a; von Soden 1969: § 12a; Hirsch 1975:293, 298). A reconsideration of the place of stress in synchronic VOWEL DELETION

---

[29] Since the vowel *i* elides, the preceding *u* in these examples must be synchronically short although it was once long. The historical derivations are: \**yawbil* > \**'uubil* > *'ubil*, \**yawrid* > \**'uurid* > *'urid*. For discussion of this problem see § 5.61 below.

shows it to be a superfluous feature. This is not surprising since stress in Akkadian is not phonemic; it follows rather than precedes VOWEL DELETION.

### 5.4.1. STRESS in Akkadian

Stress assignment, as far as we can tell, is a low-level phonological process in Akkadian (cf. Knudsen 1980:3-4). Akkadian had no diacritical system for marking accentuation in the orthography and has no living tradition of pronunciation, so we cannot be at all certain concerning the historical reconstruction of its stress system. Sarauw (1939), in one of the largest treatises on Akkadian accentuation, conceded that we know very little about Akkadian stress. For the most part, grammarians have assumed that Akkadian shared the system of accentuation that is attested in Classical Arabic (cf. Rodgers 1977: 10-30; Knudsen 1980:7-10). Basically, this rule stresses the last heavy syllable in a word (a syllable having at least three segments), or, in the absence of a heavy syllable, the first syllable of a word (e.g., Ungnad and Matouš 1969:§ 24a; Moscati 1969:§ 10.6).[30] The Arabic analogy, however, is not as firm as had been thought (cf. Knudsen 1980:10), and the Akkadian rule cannot be confirmed empirically. Orthography by itself cannot serve as an index because it is inconsistent and could deploy the doubled (*plene*) writing of vowels to represent a variety of phenomena, such as segmental length, grammatical distinctions, and the like (cf. Rodgers 1977:8-9; Knudsen 1980:10-12; see § 5.64 below; contrast Knudsen 1980:13).

#### 5.4.1.1. METRICAL EVIDENCE BEARING ON STRESS

The only avenue by which we may approach Akkadian stress directly is the analysis of poetic meter (cf. now Knudsen 1980:13-14). Landsberger (1965 [1928]:371-372) observed that every line of Akkadian verse ends in a trochee (´˘), a position which has been endorsed by many scholars (e.g., Böhl 1960:149; Held 1961:3, n. 22; 1976:234; Ungnad and Matouš 1969:§ 24c; Kuryłowicz 1972:185; Knudsen 1980:13-14). If so, a penultimate syllable at the end of a line of verse was stressed. Landsberger's theory relies not only on presuppositions regarding Akkadian accentuation and *plene* writings. Akkadian poets employed at least two artificial devices in order to ensure that lines would end in a trochaic pattern.

One is the apocopation of the last vowel in a pronominal suffix, making the antepenultimate syllable into the penultimate. The phenomenon is attested already in OAkk., e.g., *múuraš*, for *múurašu* 'its young one' (MAD 5, 8:24; see also Steiner 1979:166-167, n. 20). Examples from Standard Babylonian (references are to pages in Hecker 1974) are: *tukúltuk* (113), *biríišun* (118), *gimríišun* (121),[31] *rígmuš* (140). In each case the originally

[30] Reiner (1966:38) has dissented, contending that Akkadian stressed the first syllable of every word, as in some Slavic languages. Her proposal is supported in part for late Akkadian dialects by Kaufman (1974:148). Reiner's reasoning is highly theoretical. For example, she argues that when a short open vowel elides, it may be the second vowel of a word but never the first. A more plausible explanation for this fact, however, is that the first vowel is constrained from eliding in order to prevent the formation of a syllable-initial consonant cluster (cf. Rodgers 1977:28).

[31] The genitive vowel is not short and stressed (so, e.g. Gelb 1955:104a; Ungnad and Matouš 1969:§ 24a) but is phonologically lengthened prior to STRESS application (see § 5.63 below).

antepenultimate syllable had been the last heavy one in the word. This prosodic phenomenon of suffix-vowel apocopation is occasionally attested in prose, too; cf., e.g., *'in šigarrim 'ana bab* <sup>d</sup>*Enlil 'úuruš* "He led him in a neck-stock to the Enlil gate" (AfO 20, p. 35:25-28; OAkk.); *'ana PN ša 'aráamuš qibiima* "To PN, whom I esteem, say . . ." (PBS I/2, 67:1; MB).

The second artifice to assure a verse-final trochee is the frequent and otiose suffixation of enclitic *-ma* in Akkadian poetry (cf. Böhl 1960:151; Hecker 1974:108). Examples from En. el. IV are: *'ilíima* (lines 11, 21), *gimílma* (line 17), *purú'ma* (line 31), *halípma* (line 57), *'ušardíima* (line 59), *tešéema* (line 83), *'izaanúuma* (line 99), *'udannínma* (line 127), and *'ihíitamma* (line 141).

The poets may have used one additional technique to ensure a line-final trochee, the alteration of prosaic word order. Consider the following examples from En. el. IV. In line 9 the subject noun *seqarka* 'your command', which ends in a trochee according to the commonly held theory, is positioned after rather than before its predicate *laa saraar* 'cannot be impeached'. This contrasts with the regular word order in line 10 in which the verb phrase, *laa 'ittiq* 'will not overstep', which ends in a trochee, follows its object noun *'itukka* 'your bounds' and closes the line. Similarly, line 12 . . . *luu kuun 'ašrukka* "let (it) be in your place" and line 15 . . . *luu šaqa(a)t 'aawatka* "may your word be supreme" place the noun before its predicate and thereby create a trochaic stress at the line's end. The verb is preposed, counter to normal word order, in lines such as the following, too: . . . *'iimuruu 'iluu 'abbuušu* "the gods, his fathers, saw" (line 27); . . . *'uštaṣbitu(u)š harraanu* "they set him on a journey" (line 34). In both cases the prosaic word order would not have resulted in a trochee but the alteration produced the desired accent.

I feel more diffident about this artificial device to create a line-final trochee than about the preceding two because the evidence may be interpreted otherwise. One finds inversions of word order not only at a line's end but at its beginning, too. An example is En. el. IV:35: *'ibšimma qašta kakkašu 'u'addi* "He constructed a bow and deemed it his weapon." In the first clause the verb precedes the object-noun, which contrasts with the second clause where the verb follows the object-noun, as in prosaic order. Inverted word-order at the end of a line may also serve the function of developing a chiasm with a parallel clause at the end of the succeeding line. An example is En. el. IV:23-24:

> . . . *li''abit luwaašu*
>
> . . . *luwaašu lišlim*
>
> . . . may the constellation be destroyed.
>
> . . . may the constellation become whole.

It is still possible that the desire to produce a line-final trochee was *one* of the poetic motives for altering prosaic word order in Akkadian verse.

Some exception has been taken to the metrical theory concerning the verse-final trochee. Held (1961:3, n. 22) has expressed doubt that the supposedly short vowel of the genitive case-ending is stressed when it is located in the penultimate syllable. The doubt is unnecessary, however, because the genitive vowel is lengthened when suffixes are appended (see § 5.63 below). Hecker (1974:102ff.) has compiled a list of alleged counter-examples to the trochee theory consisting of verse-final words which he believes did not end in a trochaic accent. Some of Hecker's examples, such as *'igigi*, are highly questionable. The majority are words ending in a long ("circumflex") vowel resulting from a contraction. Kiparsky (1968, 1972a, 1973b) has shown that metrical analysis may often be obliged to operate at the morphophonemic level. Accordingly, we should probably regard the "circumflex" vowels as /V—V/ underlyingly and perhaps [V́'V] phonetically. Compare, e.g., archaic *šamáawu* with *šamúu* 'heaven' in En. el. (see further Greenstein 1977:139ff.). One can also compare phenomena like the historical split of an extra-long vowel in Samaritan Hebrew into two syllables (Ben-Ḥayyim 1979). Hecker's examples do not confute the trochee theory, they demand a more sophisticated mode of metrical analysis. Rodgers (1977:10, 22-23) advises due caution in adopting any theory of Akkadian meter, yet he offers no substantive argument against the trochee theory.

Assuming that Akkadian meter reflects the stress patterns of the colloquial language,[32] the evidence of the trochee appears to justify the view that Akkadian stressed the last heavy syllable in a word. The fact that syllable weight often attracts stress in other languages reinforces this conclusion (cf. Hooper 1972:533; 1976:206-209; Hyman 1977; Liberman and Prince 1977; Donegan and Stampe 1978; Ohsiek 1978; McCarthy 1979).

### 5.4.2. STRESS is not phonemic in Akkadian

Since Akkadian stress is predictable, it is non-phonemic and assigned by the phonological component. Even though the precise features of Akkadian stress remain hypothetical, other linguistic considerations support the premise that Akkadian STRESS is phonologically determined and not morphophonemic. For one thing, no two words are distinguished solely on the basis of stress (cf. Reiner 1966:38; contrast Hetzron 1969; for arguments against Hetzron see Greenstein 1977:51, n. 29). For another, Akkadian distinguished phonemic length, at least long vowels from short ones (cf. Reiner 1966; Kuryłowicz 1972:40 et passim; Hirsch 1975:264-268). Typological studies have shown that "Languages where both length and stress appear as distinctive features are quite exceptional, and if stress is distinctive, it is mostly supplemented by a redundant length" (Jakobson and Halle 1957:229; cf. Jakobson 1962:526-527; Kuryłowicz 1972:158-159). If so, Akkadian would not likely have distinguished phonemic stress. Akkadian STRESS seems to apply to the outputs of VOWEL DELETION and the other phonological rules.

Empirical evidence shows that STRESS plays no role in conditioning VOWEL DELETION. For an illustration, consider the underlying representations of the Akkadian participle

---

[32] Contra Sievers (1929) and Poebel (1939:73-74 et passim), more recent studies tend to view Akkadian meter as reflective of normal stress patterns (e.g., Böhl 1960:146; Kuryłowicz 1972:177-178; Knudsen 1980:13). Most modern study on metrical theory agrees that metrical patterns do indeed correspond to the stresses of the spoken language (e.g., Chatman 1965; Halle and Keyser 1966; Chapman 1973:89ff.; Kiparsky 1975; contrast, e.g., Lord 1965:37; Miller 1977). If the meter did not by and large represent normal stress patterns, the metrical pattern could never be established in the first place (cf. Chatman 1965:118-119). When the correlation between the metrical pattern and spoken stress is broken, it is the meter that is violated in order to emphasize the stressed word or phrase. Moreover, a steady, unmodified meter becomes monotonous and tedious (cf. Ciardi 1959:esp. 930-932).

(masc. sg. nom.) and stative (3 masc. sg.). Suffixation of case-marker and subjunctive *u* produces /paaris+u/ and /paris+u/, respectively. All theories of Akkadian STRESS would in both cases assign the primary word stress to the first syllable. Only in the second case, that of the stative, does the vowel *i* undergo VOWEL DELETION and elide. Stress patterns being the same, the only crucial factor distinguishing the two cases is that in the participle the preceding syllable contains a long vowel and in the stative it does not (cf. Hirsch 1975:298). Vowel length plays a determinant role in conditioning VOWEL DELETION, STRESS does not (cf. Salonen 1949:319; Gelb 1955:111a).

## 5.5. Exceptions to VOWEL DELETION in Akkadian

VOWEL DELETION need not refer to any environmental factors other than VC_CV for most cases. There are, however, certain regular exceptions to the rule.

### 5.5.1. Non-deletion of a vowel before certain consonants

#### 5.5.1.1. NON-DELETION OF *a* BEFORE *r*

It has long been observed that a short vowel, usually *a*, is constrained from eliding by a directly following *r* (e.g., Zimmern 1890:386-388; Delitzsch 1906:§ 62; Goetze 1946b; von Soden 1969:§ 12b; Ungnad and Matouš 1969:§ 7b). Well-known examples are *'išaru(m)* 'straight', *'eperu(m)* (< * *'aparum)* 'soil', *šikaru(m)* 'beer', and *zikaru(m)* 'male'. In the most extensive treatment of this phenomenon to date, Goetze (1946b:236) concluded that "all these exceptions from the general rule [of vowel deletion] have two things in common: (1) they contain all [*sic*] the vowel *a*, and this is (2) invariably followed by the consonant *r*." The vowel /a/ often shares phonetic features with the liquid /r/, and it is natural to find phonological processes in which /ar/ becomes [aa] (e.g., Jakobson 1968:14; Chafe 1970:32; Grundt 1976:60) or /r/ becomes [(r)a] or [a(r)] (e.g., Kiparsky 1972b:212; O'Bryan 1974:52-53; cf. Steiner 1976). Goetze's assertions require extension, refinement, and elaboration, through which a larger generalization emerges.

#### 5.5.1.2. NON-DELETION OF *i* BEFORE *r*

In a number of words *i*, too, is constrained from deleting before *r*. The most common ones are *labiru(m)* 'old', *nakiru(m)* 'enemy', and *nawiru(m)* 'bright' (see below). Despite the common Assyriological practice of attributing a long vowel to *labiru*, viz., **labiiru* (e.g., Oppenheim et al. 1955-   : vol. 9:26ff.), there is every reason to vocalize it *labiru*, with short *i* (cf. von Soden 1969:§ 12b note). Morphologically, the underlying base /labir/ is of a piece with other adjectives, such as /kabit/ 'heavy'. The corresponding factitive D-stem verb of /labir/ is *lubburu* 'to make old' just as the factitive for /kabit/ is *kubbutu* 'to make heavy' (cf. Goetze 1942). In late dialects the vowel *i* does syncopate, producing *labru* instead of *labiru* (e.g., Borger Esarh., p. 94: rev. 6). Were the *i* long, it would not have been apt to elide.

The noun *nakiru(m)* 'enemy' coexists with the noun *nakru(m)* 'enemy'. In OB, for example, both *nakirum* (e.g., CH epil. 27:90; RA 33, 51:13) and *nakrum* (e.g., CH epil. 28:20;

YOS 10, 11, i:25; AbB 1, 54:6) are attested (cf. von Soden 1969: § 18c; for NA see Deller 1959:46). Many Assyriologists interpret *nakirum* as a participle, with long *a*, viz., *\*naakirum*, but the assumption is unnecessary (cf. Zimmern 1890:386-388; Gelb 1955: 100b). The form *nakirum* is formed adjectively from underlying /nakir/ while *nakrum* is a primary noun, underlyingly /nakr/.

The case of *nawiru(m)* 'bright' is more problematic because the OB writing *na-PI-rum* (e.g., YOS 9, 35:38; cf. ibid.:67) could be, and has been, interpreted as *\*nawrum* (Gelb 1961b; Reiner 1964). Synchronically the underlying form of *na-PI-rum* is /nawir+um/, as the feminine *nawirtum* (e.g., AbB 1, 51:9 *na-wi-ir-ta-am*) indicates. Later writings such as MB *na-me-ru-ti* (e.g., Hinke Kudurru iv:13) and MA *na-mi-ru-ti* (e.g., JAOS 95, 610:45) corresponding to OB *na-PI-ru-tim* (e.g., LIH 97:85) show that the vowel *i* was retained preceding *r*.[33]

### 5.5.1.3. NON-DELETION OF *u* BEFORE *r*

Non-deletion of *u* preceding *r* occurs typically in early Babylonian dialects in which the feminine plural formations *'uṣuraatu, puzuraatu*, etc. are attested with the second *u* un-deleted (see § 5.241 above).

### 5.5.1.4. NON-DELETION OF VOWELS BEFORE LIQUIDS, NASALS, AND

Goetze's second point (§ 5.511) was that vowels that do not undergo VOWEL DELETION are "invariably followed by the consonant *r*." Although this assertion is valid for the most part, the earlier back in time one looks, the less it holds true. There are occasional exam-ples of words in which a vowel fails to elide preceding *l, n,* or *'*. The first two cases are exceptional, the third is not. The best example of the non-deletion of *a* before *l* is *'akalu(m)* 'food', which becomes *'aklu* during the first millennium B.C.E. (see Oppenheim et al. 1955-   , vol. 1/1:238ff. for references). Examples of words in which *a* does not elide before *n* are *ḫatanu* 'male relative by marriage', which becomes *ḫatnu* in certain dialects (see Oppenheim et al. 1955-   , vol. 6:148 for references; cf. Zimmern 1890: 386-388; von Soden 1969: § 12b note),[34] and Assyrian *ramanu(m)* 'self', which becomes *ramnu* in later periods (see von Soden 1958-81:949-950).[35] Non-deletion of a short vowel preceding *'* is regularly attested in OA and OB (cf. Gelb 1955:102b) and can be identified already in OAkk., as in *nadi'aaku* 'I have left' (Or 40,398   :rev. 4), a form likewise evi-denced in OB (AbB 1, 18:11). Other OB examples are: *kali'aaku* 'I am detained' (AbB 1, 80:13), *šame'aaku* 'I have heard' (ibid., 30:12), *liqi'am* 'take for me' (ibid., 60:18),

---

[33] For the pronunciation of */w/ as [w] and not [m] in OB and other Akkadian dialects, see Greenstein (1977:139-168).

[34] Goetze (1947c:246-247) proffers a functional explanation for the non-deletion of the second *a* in this word. He suggests that *ḫatanu* was borrowed from West Semitic and preserved the *a* in order to separate the two dentals, *t* and *n*. This does not explain, however, early attestations of *ḫatnu* beside *ḫatanu* nor the attestation of other sequences of *d/tn* in Akkadian, such as *nidnu* 'gift' (von Soden 1958-81:786b) and *matnu(m)* 'tendon' (ibid.:633b). Viewing the non-deletion of *a* in *ḫatanu* in a broader framework, therefore, seems preferable. See below.

[35] The shortness of the second *a* is ascertained, at least for Assyrian, by the fact that the vowel under-goes Assyrian VOWEL HARMONY from OA on (cf. Goetze 1947c).

*'iltaqi'akku* 'he has obtained for you' (ibid., 74:10), [*k*]*isa'am* 'brick-mantle' (AfO 12, 364: 14), and *rabi'am* 'large' (loc. cit.). In OA one finds examples of non-deletion of the vowel preceding ', such as *niqi'um* beside *niq'um* (Hirsch 1975:398), but the constraint on deletion has begun to relax, as the following examples show: *naš'akkum* 'he is bringing to you' (BIN 4, 9:9), *teb'amma* 'get up' (TCL 19, 1:19,28).

5.5.1.5. EVENTUAL RELAXATION OF 5.5.1.1. - 5.5.1.4.

In time the constraints on the deletion of vowels preceding *r, l, n,* and ' relax. The deletion of *i* before *r* in *labiru(m)* was noted above in § 5.512. The form *nawiru(m)* eventually undergoes VOWEL DELETION and results in *nawru(m)*, often written *nam-ru* (e.g., Ebeling Handerhebung, p. 50:1,9; for NA see Deller 1959:90).[36] Contrary to the claims of many (e.g., Gelb 1955:99a; 1970:74-75; Jucquois 1966:150-153), the diphthong /aw/ would not have contracted to [uu]. The contraction of diphthongs was a diachronic process that occurred for the most part in pre-literate periods of Akkadian.[37] It was not a synchronic rule of later Akkadian. In fact, it is the synchronic non-contraction of /aw/ in *nawru(m)* that reinforced its distinction from the noun *nuuru(m)* 'light', which derived historically from *\*nawru(m)* (cf. Speiser 1953:135a). For the eventual deletion of *u* preceding *r*, see § 5.241 above.

In time even the vowel *a* comes to elide preceding *r*; e.g., *zikaru* 'male' becomes *zikru* (e.g., Erra IV:56; JNES 33, 224:4c), *'ašaru* 'place' (e.g., AfO 20, 36:31; OAkk.) becomes *'ašru* (see Oppenheim et al. 1955- , vol. 1/2:456ff.),[38] *'eperu* (< *\*'aparu*) 'soil' becomes *'epru* (cf. Goetze 1946b:235, n. 2; Rainey 1974:77), *kawaru* '(earth) terrace' becomes *kawru* (see Oppenheim et al. 1955- , vol. 8:111a),[39] *šikaru* 'beer' becomes *šikru* already in OA (cf. von Soden 1958-81:1232b). Goetze (1946b:234, 237) had explained the diachronic syncopation of *a* before *r* as a result of paradigm analogy, or levelling; e.g., *kabru* (masc.) : *kabirtu* (fem.) 'thick' = *damqu* (masc.) : *damiqtu* (fem.) 'good'. In view of the eventual relaxation of related constraints on VOWEL DELETION, it is preferable to understand the later deletion of *a* before *r* similarly, as a loosening of the constraint posed by *r*. The relaxation of the exceptional constraints on the deletion of *a* preceding *l* and *n* were cited above in § 5.514. The regular blockage of VOWEL DELETION by a following ' in early dialects (see § 5.514 above) breaks down in later dialects when either the vowel preceding ' elides or the vowels flanking the ' contract.

5.5.1.6. THE HISTORICAL PATTERN THAT EMERGES FROM 5.5.1.1. - 5.5.1.5.

Taking all the above-cited phenomena into consideration, the following historical pattern emerges. Originally, any short vowel could be constrained from deleting in the context $VC_1\_C_2V$ when $C_2$ = a laryngeal ('), a liquid (*r, l*), or the nasal *n*. In very early

[36]For the interpretation of *m* as [w] see now Greenstein (1977:139-168).

[37]For Jucquois' (1966) confusion of diachronic and synchronic description in general, see Buccellati (1971).

[38]Cf. OB *'ašariš* 'to the place' (e.g., AbB I, 28:33) > *'ašriš* (references in Oppenheim et al. 1955- , vol.1/2:455b).

[39]Written *kamru*; see n. 36 above.

(pre-literate) times the restriction against *u* and *i* was gradually removed, working its way through the lexicon but exempting certain words, such as *labiru*, *nakiru*, and *nawiru*, from the innovation. This pattern of linguistic change conforms to the model proposed by Chen and Wang (1975; cf. Hooper 1976:104; Kenstowicz and Kisseberth 1979:393).

The constraint on *a* remained in force for a longer time. This is not at all surprising since *a* is widely evidenced as the most sonorous vowel and was articulated most closely to the laryngeal and perhaps to Akkadian /r/. The vowel *a* is in general "more resistant to reduction and deletion than the high vowels" (Steiner 1979:168-169, n. 27). For example, when Aramaic borrowed the month-names from Babylonian, the vowel *a* was less often reduced than *i* or *u* (Kaufman 1974:147; cf. Malone 1971:62, n. 62).

The constraints posed by the consonants following the vowel subject to deletion also form a phonological hierarchy. In historical times *n* and *l* blocked the deletion of the preceding vowel only vestigially in a few lexemes; this restriction was eventually lifted altogether. The laryngeal ' prevented VOWEL DELETION for a much longer period (cf. the role of ' in certain West Semitic languages in Steiner 1980). The phoneme /r/ blocked VOWEL DELETION until later periods, when it ceased to perform this function (see further § 5.517 below). It is possible that /r/ was phonetically realized as an uvular since it behaves as the laryngeal in preventing DELETION. In other Semitic languages, too, /r/ behaves like a guttural (cf. Moscati 1969:§ 8.25). On the other hand, a trilled /r/ may likewise lead to a lowering of the tongue, which could account for its resemblance to the laryngeal (cf. Vennemann 1972b:874). Either way VOWEL DELETION was constrained more, the lower the vowel was articulated. The phonetic picture of the hierarchies may be observed more clearly in the following diagram:

| | | | | |
|---|---|---|---|---|
| HIGHER | i | u | l | n |
| LOWER | a | | r? | ' |

The lowest vowel resists DELETION most, the consonants that produce lower articulations of the preceding vowel constrain DELETION most.

### 5.5.1.7. DISTINGUISHING PRIMARY FROM SECONDARY VOWELS BEFORE *r, l,* AND *n*

It has long been thought by some grammarians that unelided vowels preceding *r* were inserted secondarily in response to the sonority of /r/. We must differentiate, however, between original vowels that are prevented from deleting before *r* and vowels that are inserted later secondarily (cf. Gelb 1955:100b; 1961a:126-127). We have two methods of distinguishing them. The first is intra-Akkadian. If a word is attested in most dialects and, in particular, in earlier dialects without the vowel in question, we may conclude that the vowel is secondary. The word *buqlu(m)* 'malt' occurs occasionally in OA and NB as *buqulu(m)* (references in Oppenheim et al. 1955- , vol. 2:323-324). In this case we interpret the second *u* as a secondary insertion. In the case of *šipireetu* 'messages, works', the singular *šipirtu(m)* points to an original and underlying representation /šipir+aat+u/ (see further § 7). The plural *šipireetu(m)* is attested in early dialects; *šipreetu*, minus the second *i*, is attested later; and in the first millennium the form *šipireetu* is again attested (references in von Soden 1958-81: 1244-1245). An analysis that is consonant with §§ 5.511-5.516 above and in accord with the peculiarities of NA and NB phonology is as follows.

In early periods the second *i* of *šipireetu* (and analogous examples) was blocked from deleting by the following *r*. Toward the middle of the second millennium the constraint on the vowel *i* was removed, leaving elided *šipreetu*. In NA and NB there was a tendency to insert vowels preceding liquids, nasals, and sometimes other consonants, e.g., *'uzunu < 'uznu, palagu < palgu, karašu < karšu* (cf. already Brockelmann 1966 [1908]:219; for NA see Deller 1959:17ff., 41ff.).[40] Thus in early Akkadian dialects the second *i* in *šipireetu(m)* is underlying and original; in dialects of the first millennium it is phonologically inserted and secondary.

The second method for discerning secondarily inserted vowels rests on the reconstruction of Proto-Akkadian forms by historical comparison with the other Semitic languages. Often this approach will happily intersect with the first method. A case in point is the word *'eperu(m)* 'soil'. On the basis of, e.g., Amarna Canaanite (EA 141:4; 143:11) and Biblical Hebrew, **aparu* is reconstructed. As a result of the coalescence of pharyngeals and laryngeals in Akkadian and their effects on vowel quality, **aparu* becomes *'eperu(m)* in Akkadian. Accordingly, historical reconstruction shows that the second *e* is original and underlying, not secondary (cf. Goetze 1946b:235, n. 2; contrast Speiser 1967:387; Deller 1958: 161). The intra-Akkadian evidence corroborates this conclusion, as *'eperu(m)* is attested in the earlier dialects, *'epru* in the latter half of the second millennium, and *'eperu* — now with an inserted vowel — in the first millennium (references in Oppenheim et al. 1955- , vol. 4:181ff.). The historical pattern matches that of *šipreetu*, discussed above.

### 5.5.2. Foreign words as exceptions to VOWEL DELETION

Another class of exceptions to VOWEL DELETION comprises foreign words borrowed into Akkadian, mostly from Sumerian (cf. Buccellati 1971:82). Although Goetze (1946b: 236, n. 2) appealed to hypothetical differences of stress to account for the exceptional behavior of loanwords, this is unverifiable and unnecessary. Words in this category are marked in the lexicon as foreign (cf. Harms 1968:119-120; Jeffers and Lehiste 1979:149) and are thereby exempted from the rule of VOWEL DELETION. Eventually, in some dialects, a loanword may lose its foreign designation and begin to undergo VOWEL DELE-TION. For example, the second vowel in the Sumerian loanword *nuḫatimmu(m)* 'cook' remains unelided in Babylonian dialects (except OB Mari, on the periphery) until the second quarter of the first millennium when the syncopated form, *nuḫtimmu*, is encountered (references in von Soden 1958-81:801a).

Akkadian speakers exhibit an implicit knowledge of the VOWEL DELETION rule and a desire to preserve the phonetic shape of foreign words when they double the last consonant in loanwords, e.g., Sum. *giš-sal* > Akk. *gišallu* 'oar', Sum. *é-gal* > Akk. *'eekallu* 'palace', Sum. *zulum/b* > Akk. *suluppuu* 'date' (cf. Falkenstein 1960:311). By doing so

---

[40] For the secondary insertion of *a* preceding *ḫ* and *r* in MA, see Mayer (1971:§13-4). For occasional examples in various peripheral Akkadian texts, see Jucquois (1966:188-189) and Berkooz (1966 [1937]: 37). For a possible orthographic explanation of the phenomenon in NA, see Deller (1962a).

they could in many cases avert the deletion of vowels in loanwords (cf. Kaufman 1974:26, n. 70). [41]

The relationship between Sumerian and Akkadian with respect to VOWEL DELETION will be taken up again in § 5.7.

### 5.5.3. The first vowel of /CVCV/-shaped suffixes as an exception to VOWEL DELETION

The second and third person plural pronominal suffixes of Akkadian have the shape /CVCV/. When they are suffixed to noun forms that end in two underlying consonants, the rule of a-EPENTHESIS (§ 3) inserts a preceding the suffix. This creates an environment for VOWEL DELETION to apply to the first of the two suffix vowels. Except for OA (for which see § 5.531 below) this vowel does not delete; e.g., libbašunu 'their heart' (e.g., AbB I,36:17; OB), maṣṣartašunu 'their guard' (PBS I/2, 43:12; MB), libbakunu 'your heart' (AOS 6 #28: obv. 4; NA). As STRESS does not seem to be a synchronic factor in VOWEL DELETION (see § 5.4 above), we should not attribute the exception of this vowel to VOWEL DELETION to putative stress conditions. Rather, the constraint is morphologically conditioned, i.e., there is a morphological constraint on the deletion of the suffix vowel in order, perhaps, to preserve the clarity of the suffix morpheme (cf. Buccellati 1971:82). [42]

#### 5.5.3.1. VOWEL DELETION IN OLD ASSYRIAN

In OA the first vowel in pronominal suffixes of /CVCV/ shape does delete following a-EPENTHESIS, producing forms such as libbašnu 'their heart', tuppašnu 'their tablet', and tertaknu 'your order' (cf. von Soden 1969:§ 12d; Ungnad and Matouš 1969:§§ 26c, n. 5; 42d). There are several written forms in which the first suffix vowel is orthographically represented, e.g., té-er-ta-ku-nu (BIN 4, 3:17) in contrast to té-er-ták-nu (Kienast ATHE #26:12; cf. Hirsch 1967:325-326; 1975:281, n. 112). However, since the forms reflecting VOWEL DELETION predominate (documentation in Deller 1959:146-148), it is evident that the forms with the deleted vowel represent phonetic spellings and the undeleted forms represent morphophonemic spellings (cf. von Soden 1969: Erg. to § 65f). We shall now investigate the reason for which OA differs from other Akkadian dialects in deleting the first vowel of a /CVCV/ suffix.

##### 5.5.3.1.1. Stress conditions as a possible factor

Ungnad and Matouš (1969:§ 42d) hypothesize that stress shifted to the epenthetic a, e.g., libbášunu, leading to the syncopation of the vowel in the next syllable, viz., [libbášnu]. This is very unlikely because in forms like OA sinnišaatini 'you are women' (cited in ibid.:§ 54b), a long and presumably stressed vowel, áa, blocks the deletion of the suffix vowel in the succeeding syllable.

##### 5.5.3.1.2. Rule-ordering as a possible explanation

Perhaps the difference between the deletion of the suffix vowel in OA and the non-deletion of the suffix vowel in OB may be attributed to a difference in synchronic rule-

[41]For a similar historical process in Aramaic, see Cantineau (1932:128).

[42]For a recently exposed case of morphological conditioning in Hebrew phonology, see Malone (1976).

ordering. Whether rules apply simultaneously or iteratively, in a universally determined sequence or in a language-specific order, are issues which continue to occupy generative phonologists (cf., e.g., Hooper 1976:53-83, 99-101; Sommerstein 1977:177-180; Goyvaerts 1978:51-99; Iverson and Sanders 1978; Kenstowicz and Kisseberth 1979:291-330). Leaving the issue of universal (intrinsic) vs. language-specific (extrinsic) rule-ordering aside, OA evinces the need for some type of rule-ordering. For example, VOWEL DELETION must precede VOWEL HARMONY:

| /libb+šunu/ | /libb+šu/ | |
|---|---|---|
| libbašunu | libbašu | *a*-EPENTHESIS |
| libbašnu | - - - | VOWEL DELETION |
| - - - | libbušu | VOWEL HARMONY |

Otherwise, the outputs would be *libbušnu* and *libbušu*, the former of which is incorrect.

In generative theory divergence in rule-ordering may serve to differentiate dialects (cf., e.g., Halle 1964:343-344; Harms 1968:52-53; Kiparsky 1971a [1965]:25ff.; King 1969:51-58; Malone 1971; Sommerstein 1977:185; Chambers and Trudgill 1980:46-47). It is therefore plausible to theorize that in OA *a*-EPENTHESIS precedes VOWEL DELETION, while in other dialects it is the reverse. Observe the contrast in the following derivations:

*Old Assyrian*

| /libb+šunu/ | |
|---|---|
| libbašunu | *a*-EPENTHESIS |
| libbašnu | VOWEL DELETION |

*Old Babylonian*

| /libb+šunu/ | |
|---|---|
| - - - | VOWEL DELETION |
| libbašunu | *a*-EPENTHESIS |

The outputs are correct. The chief inherent difficulty with this analysis is that VOWEL DELETION gives every sign of being a "persistent rule" (Chafe 1968) in Akkadian; it keeps applying to each new environment that meets its structural description. This is suggested by the fact that VOWEL DELETION operates across strings of words as well as within morphs.

5.5.3.1.2.1. VOWEL DELETION across word boundaries. Phonetic writings that reflect VOWEL DELETION across word boundaries in compounds, genitive constructs, prepositional and other phrases, and personal names are attested in all period of Akkadian (cf., e.g., Ungnad and Matouš 1969: § § 88b, 89a, 89b, 93a; von Soden 1969: § 12e; Reiner 1973b; Finet 1956: § 7a; Mayer 1971: § 11-2; for the application to poetry see Sievers 1929:12). The following examples are illustrative: *wa-ar-dí-li-šu* = /warad+'ilii+šu/ (cited in Lewy 1938:

456); *a-té-ir-ti-ka* = /ana+teertika/ (BIN 4, 2:21; both OA)[43] ; *ri-ig-ma-*$^{ld}IM$ = [rigmadad]
= /rigim+'adad/ (YOS 10, 18:47; OB); *ša-ak-nu* $^{d}en$-*lil* = [šaknenlil] = /šakin+'enlil/
(Borger Esarh. p. 1:4-5, 8, NA); *la-ab-rat* = /labar+at(ta)/ (cited in Hirsch 1975:311, n.
246; LB); and note the Greek transcription $\varphi\alpha\rho\delta\alpha\epsilon\iota\varphi\eta$ < /parda+ina+pee/ (cited in Schileico
1928/29:13).

5.5.3.1.3.  The case of the I/2 infinitive in Old Assyrian

The difference between OA and the other dialects with respect to the deletion or non-
deletion of the first vowel in /CVCV/-shaped suffixes is not the only idiosyncrasy of OA.
The situation of the I/2 infinitive in OA may help to shed light on our problem.

In OA the I/2 infinitive takes the form *litabšum* while in OB the form is *litbušum*. Similarly, the I/2 preterite plus ventive suffix is *'atalkam* in OA but *'atlakam* in OB (cf. Ungnad
and Matouš 1969:§67c and below). Several explanations have been proffered to account
for the distinctive OA forms. One is that the difference is not phonological but lexical,
i.e., that OA inserted the infix /ta/ into these forms while OB used /t/ (cf. thus far Hecker
1968a:160). In OA underlying /litabušum/ is posited. VOWEL DELETION applies to the
third short open vowel and produces [litabšum], which is correct. In OB underlying
/litbušum/ is posited. VOWEL DELETION does not apply, and [litbušum] is the correct
output. Similarly, OA ['atalkam] can be derived by applying VOWEL DELETION to an
underlying /'atalakam/, and OB /'atlakam/ remains ['atlakam].

Though plausible, this solution encounters a number of difficulties. First, we have more
reason to posit /ta/ than /t/ as the underlying infix in OB (cf. von Soden 1969:§92a).
The morph /ta/ is more transparent, as in *'aptaris* etc., and thus more learnable. Moreover,
if /t/ is posited, a rule of epenthesis is required in addition to the independently motivated
rule of *a*-EPENTHESIS described above (§3.0; cf. also §5.241). Second, this solution does
not explain why the third and not the second of the short open vowels deletes in OA.
And third, the phenomenon seems to occur not only in verbs with an infixed /t/ or /ta/.
Contrast, e.g., the writing of the place-name Dur-Ḥumid in OA, *tur₄-ùh-mì-id*, with the
variant writing *tù-ur-ḫu-mì-id* (references in Hecker 1968a:160; 1968b:§7c). This suggests
a phonological explanation.

Von Soden (1969:§92a) derives both the OA and OB forms from the same underlying
base, viz., /litabušum/ and /'atalakam/. The OA forms, he contends, undergo a metathesis
of a vowel and a consonant, presumably after VOWEL DELETION had deleted the second
or third short open vowel. The theory succeeds in deriving forms in which the resultant
second vowel is *a*, as in *'atalkam*. It cannot, however, derive *litabšum* from /litabušum/.
If the /a/ metathesizes, the result is [litbašum], and if the /u/ metathesizes, the result is
[litubšum], both of which are incorrect.

Poebel (1939:46), too, posits identical bases for both the OA and OB forms. Character-
istically, he attributes the surface differences to differences in word stress, /litabušum/

---

[43] Contrast the morphophonemic writing in the same letter, line 4: *a-na té-ir-tí-ia*. Note that the phonetic
form of /teertika/ is [tertiika] after the phonological rules of VOWEL SHORTENING (§6) and VOWEL
LENGTHENING (§5.63) have applied.

becoming *litabšum* in OA but *litbušum* in OB (cf. Whiting 1981:11, n. 45). Aside from its questionable reliance upon phonemic stress (see § 5.4), this theory depends upon an otherwise unmotivated assumption of lexical stress differences between OA and OB. In fact, the stress differences more likely result from low-level phonological STRESS. In OA the vowel *a* is stressed because after VOWEL DELETION it belongs to a heavy (closed) syllable, and in OB the vowel *i* is stressed because after VOWEL DELETION it, too, belongs to a heavy (closed) syllable.

It is becoming clear that the reasons for the difference between the OA and OB forms involves VOWEL DELETION and hinges on the fact that in, say, /litabušum/, the vowel *a* elides in OB while the vowel *u* elides in OA (thus far Gelb 1955:110b). The VOWEL DELETION rule must include a built-in device for selecting the correct vowel on which to operate when it is confronted, as it is in this case, with two possibilities. Since the outputs in OA and OB differ, the device must obey a different principle in the two dialects. In OA the selector chooses the third of three short open vowels for deletion, and in OB it chooses the second. Generative analyses have shown elsewhere that some phonological rules must apply in a stipulated direction (cf., e.g., Sommerstein 1977:171-173; Goyvaerts 1978:82-86; Kenstowicz and Kisseberth 1979:326ff.). Here, too, we see that in OA VOWEL DELETION scans the underlying string from left to right while in OB VOWEL DELETION scans from right to left.[44] This solution produces correct derivations:

### Old Assyrian

| /'atalakam/ | /litabušum/ | /duru+ḫumid/ | |
|-------------|-------------|--------------|---|
| ['atalkam]  | [litabšum]  | [duruḫmid]   | Left-to-Right VOWEL DELETION |

### Old Babylonian

| /'atalakam/ | /litabušum/ | /duru+ḫumid/ | |
|-------------|-------------|--------------|---|
| ['atlakam]  | [litbušum]  | [durḫumid]   | Right-to-Left VOWEL DELETION |

Unfortunately, a left-to-right application of VOWEL DELETION in OA does not solve the problem of why the first vowel of /CVCV/-shaped suffixes deletes in OA but not in OB etc. (§ § 5.53-5.531). We must therefore conclude that in OA the constraint against the deletion of a suffix vowel did not obtain.

### 5.5.4.  Summary of exceptions to VOWEL DELETION

There are basically three circumstances in which VOWEL DELETION is constrained: (1) preceding a guttural or /r/, and sometimes /l/ and /n/, especially with respect to the vowel /a/; (2) in foreign words; and (3) within pronominal suffixes (except in OA).

---

[44] The crucial importance of directional rule application here and elsewhere presents a formidable challenge to those phonologists who contend that rules apply simultaneously to any underlying string.

## 5.6. VOWEL DELETION affects short vowels only

Apart from the constraints summarized in § 5.54, VOWEL DELETION is an exceptionless
rule of Akkadian phonology. We may now form certain conclusions concerning the environment and nature of vowels that do and do not undergo VOWEL DELETION. A vowel
that deletes in the context VC_CV must be short. A vowel that does not delete must be
long, unless it falls within one of the three categories of regular exceptions. If a presumably short vowel in the context VC_CV does not delete, the context must have been
described incorrectly; either one of the consonants must be geminated or the preceding
vowel must be long. Otherwise, the vowel that resists deletion must in fact be long.

### 5.6.1. Putative counterexamples discussed

The standard grammars of Akkadian include at least two items which seem to pose a
challenge to the absolute operation of VOWEL DELETION as it has been defined. One
is that when a suffix such as the ventive /am/ is appended to the verb /'ubil/ 'he brought',
VOWEL DELETION applies and produces ['ublam] 'he brought here/to me'. Historically —
and synchronically according to most grammars — the first vowel of the verb-form, /u/, is
long (see n. 29 above). Therefore, the vowel /i/ in the following syllable should not elide
(cf. von Soden 1969: § 12f; Ungnad and Matouš 1969: § 80c; Hirsch 1975:278, n. 92). I
agree that the first vowel should be reconstructed as long. In OAkk., in fact, the /i/ is
written undeleted, i.e., as 'uubilam. However, already in OAkk. texts, and thereafter, the
form 'ublam occurs (cf. Gelb 1955:111a; 1961a:126). What appears to have happened is
that through casual speech or some other cause the vowel /i/ began to elide exceptionally.
The resultant form *'uublam then became subject to the rule of VOWEL SHORTENING,
which shortens a long vowel in a closed syllable (see § 6 below), yielding 'ublam. The
vowel /u/ was then reinterpreted (§ 1.41) as a short vowel underlyingly. As a result, the
reanalyzed base form, /'ubil/, became subject to VOWEL DELETION when a vowel was
suffixed (cf. Hecker 1968b: § 93c; contrast Hirsch 1972:404). The allo-form 'ublam beside
'ubil, therefore, constitutes no exception to the VOWEL DELETION rule. The analogous
diachronic development of beltu(m) from beeletum 'lady' will be discussed below.

The second question concerns the phonological shape of the present form of quadriliteral
verb-stems of the type nabalkutu(m) 'to revolt'. Ungnad and Matouš (1969: § 73c) list the
form as 'ibbalakkat, in which no segment would be subject to VOWEL DELETION. The
standard treatise on quadriliteral verbs by Heidel (1940:119 et passim), however, under-
stands the form as 'ibbalakkat, with secondary doubling of /k/ attributed to stress. [45] We
may infer that in Heidel's view the underlying form is /'in(a)balakat/, in which case the
second or third /a/ should undergo VOWEL DELETION, regardless of stress conditions.
Heidel assumed that the second a was secondary and not morphophonemic on the basis
of a late diachronic development, attested especially in NA, [46] in which the present
'ibbalak(k)at becomes what he takes to be 'ibbalkat. This reading of the form was based

---

[45] Heidel (1940) also follows Poebel (1939) in analyzing the G-stem present as 'ipár(r)as, a view which
is rarely considered nowadays.

[46] Gordon (1938:35) cites a form i-ba-qa-tu$_4$ (='ibbakkatu) beside i-ba-la-ka-tu$_4$ (='ibbalakkatu) in Nuzi
Akkadian.

on writings such as *i-BAL-ka-ta* (AOS 6 #13: rev. 11), *i-BAL-kat-u-ni* (Postgate NA Leg. Docs. 19:20), and *ib-BAL-kàt-u-ni* (ibid. 47:16). But the same form can be written *ib-bal-lak-kàt-u-ni* (ibid. 46:9) or *i-ba-la-kàt-u-ni* (references in Deller 1959:3; 1962b:8-9), indicating a phonetic [a] preceding the [kk]. Through orthographies such as these Deller (1962b) has demonstrated that many CVC-signs in the NA syllabary have the additional value CVCV. The proper reading of the *BAL*-sign in forms such as *i-BAL-kat* is *bala*. The underlying form */ˈin(a)balakat/ that Heidel imputed is, consequently, erroneous, and the correct underlying representation, /ˈin(a)balakkat/, is not subject to VOWEL DELETION.

### 5.6.2. Putative long vowels that are actually short

The application or non-application of VOWEL DELETION is one of the surest means of determining synchronic length in Akkadian phonology. This principle, together with the operation of Assyrian VOWEL HARMONY (see n. 48 below), was utilized for this purpose by Goetze (1947c). As a result of this technique many Akkadian words can be vocalized on a more sound empirical basis. For example, the word for 'word' is vocalized by von Soden (1969: § 15d) as [ˈawaatu(m)]. The allegedly long vowel, however, undergoes Assyrian VOWEL HARMONY and must, accordingly, be short (Goetze 1947c:244-245). Well aware of this, von Soden conceded that the second vowel was short in Assyrian but not in Babylonian. There is no reason to prevent us from vocalizing the Babylonian form as [ˈaawatu(m)], however (cf. also Kraus 1976:293). A long vowel in the first syllable restrains VOWEL DELETION from applying to a short vowel in the succeeding syllable.

### 5.6.3. VOWEL LENGTHENING in Akkadian

One condition in which VOWEL DELETION fails to apply testifies to another rule of Akkadian morphophonology. When a suffix beginning with a consonant is attached to a morph ending in a vowel, that vowel does not undergo VOWEL DELETION in the context VC_CV. Grammarians have properly inferred that the vowel is long (e.g., Ryckmans 1938: § 36 bis; Ungnad and Matouš 1969: § § 8b, 83d note). However, they generally assume that this vowel is long as a secondary result of STRESS (e.g., Delitzsch 1906: § 66d; Sarauw 1939:12; von Soden 1969: § § 15c, 65a; Ungnad and Matouš 1969: § 42a). As I have argued above (§ 5.4 et passim), this assumption places the cart before the horse. If stress falls on that syllable it is because the vowel is underlyingly long and the syllable, as a result, heavy.

In some cases the undeleted vowel appears to be etymologically long, as in *'abuuša* 'her father' (AbB I, 51:23), *'emuušu* 'his father-in-law' (LE § 25:26), and *'aḫaašu* 'his brother' (Lambert-Millard Atra-ḫasīs p. 94:13-14; all OB). Contrast *'aḫša* 'her arm' (AbB I, 53:26).[47] The words *ʾabu, *ʾaḫu, and *ʾamu are treated as final-weak stems in Semitic (e.g., Nöldeke 1910:112; Barth 1887:609-612; Speiser 1953:132b). Another example is the vocalic desinence of all 3rd person plural verb forms (cf., e.g., Moscati 1969: § § 16.41, 16.61).

In several morphological positions, however, the undeleted vowel appears to be originally short. Consider the following cases.

---

[47] For *'aḫšu* 'his brother' in Assyrian, see Deller (1965:79).

(a)   When pronominal suffixes are attached to the final vowel of final-weak prepositions, e.g., *biri*, the vowel /i/ does not elide: *biriini* 'between us' (EA 7:39; MB).

(b)   The "subjunctive" marker *u* does not elide when followed by a pronominal suffix or enclitic *-ma*: *'iddinuušum* '(which) he gave to him' (MCS 4, 13: obv. 11; OAkk.), *'ušakliluušu* 'whom he perfected' (CH prolog 3:27; OB).

(c)   The final vowel of final-weak verbs does not elide when a suffix is attached: *nidiima* 'it is deposited' (stative; BIN 4, 4:9; OA), *qibiima* 'speak!' (passim), *'iqtabiišunu* 'he has spoken of them' (EA 29:173; Mitanni MB).

(d)   Final vowels of pronouns and pronominal suffixes do not elide when followed by enclitic *-ma*: *šunuuma* 'they' (TCL 20, 111:14), *šašqilaašunuuma* 'pay them' (ibid. 16:18; OA), *waradkunuuma* 'your (pl.) slave' (AbB 1, 29:3; OB).

(e)   The genitive ending /i/ does not elide when suffixes are added: *naphariišunu* 'all of them' (JNES 31, 334:16; OAkk.), *šaapiriini* 'our chief' (AbB 1, 25:obv. 1), *'aššumiini* 'concerning us' (ibid. 45:4; OB), *'aššatiika* 'your wife' (EA 10:4; MB), *paalihiišu* 'his devotee' (AOS 6 #12: obv. 15; NA). The length of genitive /i/ when followed by a suffix is corroborated by the fact that it does not undergo VOWEL HARMONY in Assyrian. [48]   Contrast *'ina libbiika* 'in your heart' (Kienast ATHE #30:21-22) with *libbušu* 'his heart' (ibid. #36:8) and *libbaka* 'your heart' (ibid. #43:31). Although some have maintained that the genitive suffix in the singular was historically long in contrast to the nominative and accusative, there is good reason to believe it was short (cf., e.g., Moscati 1969: § 12.64).

In all five cases (a through e) an underlyingly short vowel does not delete, meaning that the vowel somehow became long (see § 5.6). Our method (§ 1.4) dictates that we seek a unitary explanation. The most straightforward solution is to deduce that Akkadian possessed a rule that lengthened the vowel in each case. We may formulate the rule of VOWEL LENGTHENING as follows:

> Lengthen a morph-final vowel when a consonant-initial morpheme
> is suffixed to it.

The rule may well have arisen to serve a functional need: to prevent the application of VOWEL DELETION and to thereby render the various forms more transparent.

The consistent application of the VOWEL DELETION rule to appropriate environments is, then, the optimum means of determining which vowels are synchronically long or short in Akkadian.

---

[48] The Assyrian rule of VOWEL HARMONY may be formulated as follows: A short open vowel, usually /a/, in the penultimate syllable of a word acquires the features of a vowel in the following syllable. For the various aspects of this rule see: Deller (1959:5ff., 145ff., 196ff.), von Soden (1969: § 10e), Ungnad and Matouš (1969: § 5b), Hirsch (1975:273, n. 71), Moran (1978:72a). Reference to stress conditions is unnecessary and redundant. Note, e.g., the effect of the case marker in the word for 'ground': *qaqquru* (nom.), *qaqqiri* (gen.), *qaqqara* (acc.) (references in Deller 1969:48).

### 5.6.4. The unreliability of cuneiform orthography as an indicator of vowel length

The reliability of VOWEL DELETION to identify certain vowels as long or short (§ § 5.6-5.63) contrasts markedly with the inconsistency and unreliability of Akkadian orthography as an indicator of vowel length. Yet, the addition of a vowel grapheme in cuneiform, a so-called *"plene"* writing, is commonly interpreted as a representation of vowel length (e.g., Speiser 1941: § 22; Aro 1953:esp. 7-8; Jucquois 1966:160ff.; Lieberman 1977:23, n. 57). Following this methodology, to confirm the rule of VOWEL LENGTHENING which we have just established (§ 5.63), for example, one would adduce instances of *plene* writing such as *ku-nu-ki-i-[šu]* 'his seal' (AbB 1, 46:13), *it-ti-i-ka* 'with you' (ibid. 56:8), *i-na-ṭà-lu-ka-a-ma* 'they will observe you' (ibid. 36:16), and the like. This approach, however, does not reckon with the fact that such writings are exceptional. In both early and late periods of Akkadian, *plene* writing of long vowels is less common than "defective," non-*plene* writings (e.g., Gelb 1955:97; 1969:22; Reiner 1966:42).

It cannot be denied that *plene* spellings often correspond to linguistically determined long vowels. But the same vowel may be written both *plene* and defectively within the same corpus. Contrast, e.g., OB *ša-al-ma-ta* (AbB 1, 4:6) with *[š]a-al-ma-a-ta* (ibid. 5:7) = [šalmaata] 'you are well'; MB *ši-ip-ri-ka* (EA 11:rev. 32) with *ši-ip-ri-i-ka* (ibid. :9) = [šipriika] 'your message' (gen.); NA *kal-bi-šu* = [kalbiišu] 'his dog', *ma-ar-i-šu* = [maariišu] 'his son' with *ma-ti-i-ka* = [maatiika] 'your land', *qab-le-e-ka* =[qableeka] 'your battle' (references in Deller 1969:48). [49] One might claim that where long vowels are written both *plene* and defectively, one relies on the *plene* spellings as phonetically revealing. This implies, however, that *plene* writing purports to indicate vocalic length (contrast already Ryckmans 1938: § 11). Such an assumption can lead to faulty methodology and erroneous conclusions.

For one thing, *plene* writings sometimes represent vowels that can in no way be defended as long. In the OB omen collection (YOS 10), for example, the final vowel of pronominal suffixes is frequently written *plene*, as in *-ka-a, -šu-ú*, etc. (references in Nougayrol 1950: 112, n. 8). There are cases in OB in which short epenthetic *a* is written *plene* (references in Aro 1971:248-249). These "abnormal" spellings (Aro 1953, 1955:26-31, 1971:248-252) indicate that vocalic length cannot be induced from *plene* writing.

*Plene* writing of vowels may represent a variety of phenomena besides phonological length. An extra vowel grapheme may be used to indicate a glottal stop word-initially (see n. 4 above) or intervocalically, particularly in early dialects: *a-aḫ-ša* 'her arm' (AbB 1, 53:26), *e-ez-ba-am* 'it was left' (ibid. 21:21), *še-a-am* = [še'am] 'barley' (Iraq 38, 57:9) (cf. Jucquois 1966:164, 175-181; Knudsen 1980:10-11). The sequence *a-a* frequently indicates an intervocalic glide, e.g., [ay(y)a] (e.g., Hirsch 1975:265-266). The *plene* writing of a word-final vowel may indicate a rise in intonation (e.g., Aro 1953:6; Knudsen 1980:11). In particular, it has been maintained that the *plene* spelling of a vowel may represent the presence of stress on that syllable (e.g., Sarauw 1939:53 et passim; Poebel 1939:60,

---

[49] For inconsistent spellings of this type in Mari OB, see Finet (1956: § 1a); for OB in general, see Aro (1971:248-249); for peripheral MB, see Jucquois (1966:163). For OB writings of contracted vowels, see Aro (1953:5); for MB, see Aro (1955:26-31).

141-142 et passim; Aro 1953:18; Deller 1959:188ff.; Jucquois 1966:175-176; von Soden 1969: § § 20e,g; Aro 1971:250; Parpola 1974:7,10,nn.11-12; Knudsen 1980:13). From the orthography alone it cannot be ascertained whether a *plene* writing represents a phonologically long vowel, a prosodic feature, or no phonological phenomenon at all. We should be prepared to admit that *plene* writings reflect scribal predilections or plain errors at least some of the time (cf. Gelb 1955:108b).

One wonders, for example, what phenomenon could be represented by the spellings *da-mi-i-iq* 'it is good' and *le-e-em-nu-um* 'bad' in OB (cited in Aro 1971:249). If *damiq* were stressed on the second syllable, *lemnum* should be so stressed. Or, if *damiq* were to reflect a lexical stress, viz., /damíq/, *lemnum* should be so stressed underlyingly, viz., /lemún+um/, and be exempted from VOWEL DELETION, which it is not. Obviously, *plene* writing is at best an uncertain guide to any particular phenomenon.

Because *plene* writings are inconsistently used, it is unlikely that they originated in order to render a phonetic feature such as vocalic length or stress (cf. Sarauw 1939:51). There is some reason to suspect that the major factor in the development of *plene* spelling was not phonological but semantic: to differentiate morphological forms that would otherwise look the same (cf. Aro 1953:5 on the singular/plural distinction). Thus, already in OAkk. the plural of *'aawatum* 'word, matter' (see § 5.62), *'aawaatu(m)*, is written *a-wa-a-ti* (oblique case; JNES 31, 334, A708:18); in OB (and earlier) the plural of *'awiilum* 'man' is spelled *a-wi-le-e* = ['awiilee] (oblique; AbB I, 14:1; JCS 2, 97, #24:3). The distinction of plural from singular is preserved in writing until late times; cf. the following (literary) NB fem. plural forms: *be-li-e-ti* (ArOr 17, 187:25), *i-la-á-ti* (ibid.:26), *kib-ra-a-ti* (ibid.:30). In CH fem. plurals are commonly written *plene*, but the present form of middle-weak verbs, in which semantic confusion does not inhere, are not normally written *plene* (Poebel 1939:11). *Plene* writing, then, cannot be assumed to indicate vocalic length in these cases. Note that in the above-cited forms, *a-wa-a-ti* and *a-wi-le-e*, only the second long vowel, which serves a morphological function, is written *plene*.

## 5.7  The Sumerian origin of Akkadian VOWEL DELETION

Many languages possess rules that delete and/or reduce vowels in certain phonemic contexts. It is a bit startling to a Semitist, however, to find that a rule of VOWEL DELETION had developed in Akkadian by the middle of the third millennium B.C.E. when the syncopation of short internal open vowels did not occur in the West Semitic languages before the first millennium B.C.E. (For the deletion and reduction of short open vowels in Hebrew and Aramaic, see esp. Cantineau 1932.) Although the West Semitic evidence may not seem conclusive since it is written in a largely consonantal script, it is possible to establish the non-deletion of short vowels in the context VC_CV through the direct testimony of Amarna Canaanite and indirect induction from Ugaritic, both from about the 14th C.

In Amarna the Canaanite gloss *ha-zi-ri* (EA 138:130) = *'aṣira* 'it was restrained' shows an unelided vowel. In Ugaritic /b/ devoiced to [p] when followed by a voiceless consonant (see Greenstein 1976:51-52). Note that in the following passage the verb *\*labiša* 'he wears' occurs with voiced [b], indicating an unelided vowel in the second syllable, whereas the noun *\*lubšu* (or *\*libšu*) displays a /b/ devoiced to [p], viz., *lpš*:

*klbš. km. lpš. dm a[ḥḥ]*

*km. all. dm. aryh* (CTA 12.2.47-48)

When (Baal) wears the blood of [his bro]thers as a garment,

The blood of his kinsmen as a robe.

It is possible that Akkadian developed its rule of VOWEL DELETION through exclusively internal pressures. On the other hand, there are very strong reasons to attribute the VOWEL DELETION rule to the influence of Sumerian, a non-Semitic language which southern Mesopotamians spoke together with Akkadian for centuries during the third millennium and perhaps into the second (cf. Lieberman 1977:18-21, esp. n.50). Hundreds of words were borrowed from Sumerian into Akkadian, which Lieberman's (1977) study of OB ably documents. It is typical for phonological change to transpire in bilingual situations, like the Sumero-Akkadian one, in which there is a great deal of lexical interchange (cf., e.g., Jeffers and Lehiste 1979:151), and Sumerian influence on Akkadian phonology has already been widely acknowledged in the merger of the Semitic gutturals to /'/ in Akkadian. Since we know Akkadian only after it had come into close contact with Sumerian (cf. Lieberman 1977:17), the emergence of VOWEL DELETION may well have been stimulated by Sumerian - if Sumerian evinced such a phonological process.

A comparison of Sumerian words with their etymons reveals the clear operation of a process of VOWEL DELETION, even though it does not apply universally and even though the conditions in which it operates are not entirely known.[50] Consider the following examples (evidence in Poebel 1923, Poebel 1939, Falkenstein 1964, Lieberman 1977):

|              |              |
|--------------|--------------|
| *abariga     | abrig        |
| *agarig      | agrig        |
| *ašita       | ašte         |
| *azalag      | azlag        |
| *banigin     | bangin       |
| *birbire     | bibre        |
| *ganapanag   | ganpanag     |
| *giridu      | girdu        |
| *girgiri     | gigri        |
| *giššukara   | gišukra      |
| *ḥalapia     | ḥalpia       |
| *ḥalazura    | ḥalzura      |
| *igišedu     | igeštu       |
| *kalaga      | kalga        |

[50] I thank Dr. Stephen Lieberman for having discussed Sumerian vowel elision with me and for having corroborated its existence, despite the apparent uncertainty of the grammars.

| | |
|---|---|
| *kigala | kigla |
| *kisikil | kiskil |
| *lamaḫusa | lamḫusa |
| *muduru | mudra |
| *namerim | namri |
| *nitadam | nitlam |
| *šemesala | šemsala |
| *suḫsuḫe | sisḫe |
| *zalaga | zalga |

Although other phonological factors (such as the reduction of geminate clusters) are also involved in some of these changes, the elision of the second short open vowel is apparent (except in *igeštu*, where the process of deletion operated right-to-left rather than left-to-right as in the other examples).

In borrowing some of these and other Sumerian words, Akkadian often preserves the vowel that is apocopated in Sumerian either by exempting it from VOWEL DELETION (see § 5.52), as in *giriduum* 'canal' (Lieberman 1977:301-302), or by geminating a consonant and protecting the vowel from deletion in a closed syllable (see loc. cit.), as in *šemiššalum* 'an aromatic plant' (ibid.:482). On the other hand, the shape of the loanword in Akkadian frequently reflects the prior elision of the Sumerian vowel, e.g., Sum.*barugal* > *burgal* > Akk. *parkallum* 'seal-cutter' (ibid.:176), Sum. *gešerin* > *gešrin* > Akk. *gešrinnum* 'balance' (ibid.:294).

## 6. THE RULE OF VOWEL SHORTENING

As far as I can ascertain, Akkadian possessed a phonological rule of VOWEL SHORTENING, which we may formulate as follows:

Delete a vowel segment in the environment V_CC.

This rule has been recognized by a number of studies (e.g., Ryckmans 1938: § 35; Reiner 1966:44-46; Ungnad and Matouš 1969: § § 8a, 23, 60a), but it has been challenged by many others (e.g., Jucquois 1966:277; von Soden 1969: § § 54k, 55h et passim; Edzard 1969:83b; Wevers 1969:291b; Hirsch 1975:278; Janssens 1975:280). The rule cannot be confirmed empirically since we have no native speakers and the cuneiform orthography is ambiguous (cf. § 5.64). Two types of indirect evidence favor the assumption of the rule's existence: inferences from better known aspects of Akkadian phonology and the existence of such a rule in Semitic and other languages whose syllable structure resembles that of Akkadian.

VOWEL SHORTENING is implied by the interactions of certain phonological processes of Akkadian. For one thing, some dialects show a change of *VVC* to *VCC* and of *VCC* to *VVC* (cf., e.g., Reiner 1966:45; von Soden 1969:§ 20d; Hirsch 1975:265, for verbal forms; for OB: Goetze 1948:94; Moscati 1969:§ 10.4; for NA: Deller 1959:169ff.; for NB: *'ušeššib* < *\*ušeešib* [JAOS 95, 371:rev. 4; 372:rev. 14], etc.; contrast Hecker 1968a: 160-161). Since *CVCC* is clearly an impermissible syllable structure, perhaps *CVVC* is, too. To carry the argument further: /VVC/ and /VCC/ act as functionally equivalent environments in blocking the deletion of an  open vowel in the following syllable. The implication of this fact is not hard to draw. VOWEL DELETION fails to apply when it would create an impermissible syllable. Were a vowel to delete in the context /VCC_C/, a syllable of the shape [CVCC], a unit of four segments, would arise. VOWEL DELE-TION also fails to apply in the context /VC_CCV/. If it did, a syllable of the shape [CCV] or [CVCC] would emerge. Clearly, *CVCC* and *CCV* are both impermissible syllable structures in Akkadian. By implication, since the context /VVC_CV/ also constrains VOWEL DELETION, the syllables that would result, [CCV] or [CVVC], are impermissible. It seems that *CVVC* is an impermissible shape just as *CVCC* is and for the same reason: Akkadian does not tolerate syllables of four segments. The rule of VOWEL SHORTENING is desiderated to reduce underlying syllables of the shape /CVVC/ to [CVC], just as *a*-EPENTHESIS (§ 3) serves to convert underlying /CVCCCV/ (= /VCC$CV/ or /VC$CCV/) to an allowable sequence: [CVC$CV$CV] ($ signifies a syllable boundary).

Such a rule of VOWEL SHORTENING is widely attested in West Semitic (e.g., Brockel-mann 1966 [1908]:63; Leslau 1942:8-9; Bravmann 1977 [1953]:135; Fischer 1969:66; Malone 1971b:412 with n.66; Brame 1972:43; Hetzron 1974:6-13; Aristar 1979). More-over, such a rule is typically found in non-Semitic languages that exhibit rules of epen-thesis and vowel deletion similar to those of Akkadian (cf., e.g., Kisseberth 1970b; 1972: 204-205; Kenstowicz and Pyle 1973:28; O'Bryan 1974:50; Kenstowicz and Kisseberth 1979:83-85). These languages, like Akkadian and West Semitic, tend to avert configura-tions of [VVC] as they do sequences of [VCC], which is to say they do not allow syllables of more than three segments.

In some West Semitic languages the final syllable of a word, when stressed, may contain the sequence [VVC]. This is probably a secondary consequence of stress, as the lengthen-ing of final syllables is a common prosodic effect (cf. MacNeilage and Ladefoged 1976: 99). It is possible that the same exception obtained in Akkadian. The exception in West Semitic jibes squarely with another one: some West Semitic languages permit [VCC] in word-final position in certain words and morphological positions, as in Hebrew [nerd] 'nard' and [yɔɔlaðt] 'you (fem. sg) have given birth'. In each case a syllable possessing four segments is permitted in word-final position (only).

## 7. THE MORPHOLOGICAL RULES OF FEMININE SUFFIX SELECTION

### 7.1 Synchronic proposals

Feminine nouns in Akkadian are of one of two morphological types, those that show a suffix *t* on the surface (e.g., *biltu* 'tribute') and those that show a suffix *at* on the sur-face (e.g., *šarratu* 'queen'). Those who assume there were two suffix morphs have proposed quite a number of rules to produce the various feminine noun-forms in Akkadian:

(i)   Use the suffix /at/ if the stem to which it is attached ends in /CC/ (Brockelmann 1903:14; Ungnad and Matouš 1969: § 37c; von Soden 1969: § 60b).

(ii)   Use /at/ if the stem is monosyllabic (Ungnad and Matouš 1969: § 42f).

(iii)   Use /at/ if the stem-vowel is /a/, as in *qatl* (von Soden 1969: § 60b; Janssens 1975/76:278).

(iv)   Use /t/ if the stem is biconsonantal, i.e., monosyllabic (Brockelmann 1966 [1908]:407-408; Ungnad and Matouš 1969: § 38i).

(v)   Use /t/ if the stem is disyllabic with short vowels, e.g., *qatal* (Brockelmann 1966 [1908]:407-408).

(vi)   Use /t/ if the stem is disyllabic and has a long vowel following the first or second radical (collapsing two rules in Brockelmann 1966 [1908]:407-408).

(vii)  Use /t/ if the stem has a prefix, e.g., *narkabtu* 'chariot' (loc. cit.).

(viii) Use /t/ following a vowel (loc. cit.; Lewy 1949:117, n.53).

(ix)   Use /t/ if the stem-vowel is /i/ or /u/, i.e., *qitl* or *qutl* (von Soden 1969: § 60b; Janssens 1975/76:278).

(x)   Use /t/ if the stem is monosyllabic and has an originally long stem-vowel (Goetze 1947c:246).

There are many ways in which these rules are inadequate. As a set, rules (i), (ii), (iii), (iv), (ix), and (x) overlap; rule (ii) and rules (iv), (ix), and (x) are contradictory; rules (v), (vi), and (vii) are redundant. Some of the rules are intrinsically problematic. For example, rules (iii) and (ix) do not explain why in a word like *kalbatu* 'bitch' the *a* is part of the suffix (according to iii) while in *pirištu* 'secret' the second *i* is epenthetic (according to ix) (cf. Hirsch 1975:306). If the underlying representation of the stem of *pirištu* is /pirs/ and not /piris/, [51] we would expect the /at/ suffix to be selected so as to avert the necessity of an extra phonological process, epenthesis, to insert /i/ between /r/ and /s/. Moreover, there are a number of exceptions to (iii) such as *šalamtu* 'corpse', *napšatu* 'life', etc., which will be reconsidered below. [52] Rule (iv) necessitates that we posit underlying */šant/ for *šattu* 'year', construct *šanat*, instead of simpler /šanat/. Rule (vi) works for some derivations but not for others. For example, Brockelmann (1966 [1908]:407-408) posits an underlying /'aalid+t+u/ → ['aalittu] 'progenitress' despite the construct *'aalidat*, which points to underlying /'aalid+at+u/ instead. The surface form ['aalittu] can then be derived as follows:

/'aalid+at+u/

'aalidtu          VOWEL DELETION

---

[51] /s/ becomes [š] preceding a dental; see, e.g., Borger (1957:190, n. 1), Held (1959:173), Reiner (1966:114), Edzard (1969:83b).

[52] The explanation of Gelb (1955:107a) that "the difference between *kalbatum* and *rapaštum* is that between primary nouns and verbal nouns" has some historical validity but is synchronically superfluous and accounts for only a subset of the exceptions.

['aalittu]     HOMORGANIC CONSONANT ASSIMILATION
(see Greenstein 1980:55-56 with n.35)

Finally, these rules are inadequate because they fail to capture certain phonological generalizations and to relate FEMININE SUFFIX SELECTION to other rules of Akkadian grammar. Thus, forms to which (ii) applies generally undergo the VOWEL DELETION rule when further vocalic suffixes are appended; e.g., *'amtu* 'bondswoman', construct *'amat*, 'my bondswoman' = *'amtii*. Stems that take the suffix /at/, therefore, preserve [at] in construct (see further below). Stems that take /t/ have construct forms ending in an additional *i via i*-ADDITION (§ 4). The stems to which rules (iv), (v), (vi), (vii), (ix) — if it were correctly formulated — and (x) apply have the common property that they end in a single consonant. An adequate description of the rules governing the selection of /at/ or /t/ should express these and any other generalizations concerning the data.

## 7.2. Diachronic explanations

The main reason that the rules summarized in § 7.1 above are inadequate is that they reflect diachronic explanations of how this and that stem wound up with the suffix it did. In fact, there are three prevailing views about the identity of the feminine suffix on Akkadian nouns, and each reverberates a proposal for identifying the feminine suffix in Proto-Semitic. We shall survey the major diachronic views here.

One position, championed in particular by Brockelmann (1903a, 1903b, 1966 [1908]: 405, 408; cf. Zimmern 1890:372-373, 378; Goetze 1946a:187, n.9; Janssens 1975/76: 278), reconstructs only one suffix, *at*, though Brockelmann recognized a few basic words such as *\*bint* 'daughter' that were exceptional and had an original *t* suffix.[53] The suffix /at/ continued to be a productive nominal formative in Semitic (cf. Cohen 1970:43-47; Ambros 1969). Since many Semitic words show only *t* on the surface, Brockelmann derived them from original forms with *at* by assuming ad hoc diachronic processes of vowel syncopation had applied to the historical forms (cf. Kuryłowicz 1972:135). Unfortunately, this theory allowed for many exceptions or incorrect forms, and in order to cover them Brockelmann invoked widespread and ad hoc operations of analogy.

The historical view of positing only *at* as the original Proto-Semitic suffix finds its synchronic counterpart in the Akkadian grammars of Delitzsch (1906: § § 45a, 45b, 94), Ryckmans (1938: § § 159:161), and others. Our study of synchronic VOWEL DELETION in Akkadian (§ 5), however, explains our differences with this posture. Another synchronic theory posits only one suffix in Akkadian, but it is /t/ rather than /at/. In forms which show [a] preceding the [t] on the surface, a rule of epenthesis is applied (e.g., Diakonoff 1965:60; Reiner 1966:119). This rule does not conform in each case to the rule of *a*-EPENTHESIS, as we have described it in § 3 above. Moreover, Reiner (1966:125; cf. Ungnad and Matouš 1969: § 38j; Janssens 1975/76:282) must posit allomorphic stems for

---

[53] Speiser (1967:429, 442-443, n. 30) posits original *\*bin+at* for this word, but his argument ignores crucial phonological factors.

many feminine nouns, such as /šatt/ beside /šanat/ 'year', which complicates the grammar and overloads the lexicon. By positing underlying /šanat/ alone (cf. Goetze 1947c:240) all other forms can be derived by the independently motivated rules, e.g.:

| | |
|---|---|
| /šanat+i+šu/ | 'his year' (gen.) |
| šanatiišu | VOWEL LENGTHENING (§ 5.63) |
| šantiišu | VOWEL DELETION (§ 5) |
| [šattiišu] | nC ASSIMILATION (n. 17 above). |

There may in fact be reason for the identification of the original suffix as *t. Forms with at might have evolved from forms with original t by a diachronic epenthesis of a preceding it. Two considerations lend support to this possibility. First, t alone can be reconstructed as the feminine marker for the African branches of Afroasiatic, from which Semitic stems (e.g., Greenberg 1960; Castellino 1962:33; Speiser 1967:429). Second, synchronic rules often reflect diachronic processes in the history of a language (§ 1.4), and the synchronic rule of a-EPENTHESIS (§ 3) may reflect such a process. On the other hand, this argument is complicated by the fact that certain words in Akkadian with the suffix t correspond to words in other Semitic languages with the suffix at; e.g., Akk. 'ešertu 'ten' = Arabic 'ašaratun, Hebrew 'ăśɔɔrɔɔ (< *'ašaratu) (cf. Goetze 1946a:187, n. 13; Bravemann 1977 [1938]:17-20; Steiner 1975). This suggests that two suffixes, at and t, may have always existed in Semitic.

Indeed, another perspective on Proto-Semitic reconstructs two feminine suffix morphs, at and t (e.g., Barth 1967 [1894]:88 et passim; 1903a; 1903b; Gray 1934: §§ 57, 66, 179; Speiser 1967:420-421, 438 et passim; Greenberg 1960:321). This view holds that no general processes could have derived all cases of t from at in a consistent manner and that the rules regarding the synchronic selection of /at/ or /t/ varied among the Semitic languages (cf. Barth 1903a:635). Diachronic theories to explain the choice of at or t were proposed; for example, Barth (1887:604ff.) observed that final-weak triconsonantal stems took t, and Nöldeke (1910:124-127, 127-129 et passim) reconstructed an original at suffix for biconsonantal stems.[54] From a synchronic standpoint Brockelmann (1966 [1908]:405-408) agreed that each Semitic language had its own rules for selecting /at/ or /t/, and we shall find this to be true of Akkadian. The various rules cited in § 7.1 stem from diachronic observations such as those of Barth and Nöldeke just mentioned. But as we shall see, synchronic analysis need not consider the variety of diachronic situations and produces a far simpler set of rules.


### 7.3. The problem of alternant forms

Any theory of Akkadian that posits two underlying feminine suffix morphs, /at/ and /t/, and specific rules governing their selection must explain a perplexity: some stems seem to

[54] On the origin of Heb. [dɛlɛϑ] 'door' cf. Barth (1887:607, n. 7); contrast Huizinga (1891:53). Kuryłowicz (1972:14, n. 19) maintains that *t was the original suffix but that at was morphologized and made into a productive suffix. Yet another view, that of Gelb (1955:107a; 1965:75; 1969:3, 13, 34ff. et passim) reconstructs the Proto-Semitic feminine marker as *a. For critiques of this argument see von Soden (1970:203-204) and Greenstein (1977:91-93).

take either one, that is to say, both. Compare, e.g., *napištu* and *napšatu* 'life', *damiqtu* and *damqatu* 'good', *kabattu* and *kabtatu* 'liver', *beltu* and *beeletu* 'lady'. In response to this problem Reiner (1966:120) posits only /t/ as the feminine morph and attributes the different forms to "alternant shapes" of the stem. She must also enlist a rule of epenthesis to insert [a] preceding the /t/, but I shall explain the unacceptability of this proposal in §7.51. I shall propose a different solution to the overall problem of alternant forms in §7.7 below in accordance with the theory that there are two suffix morphs.

## 7.4. The data for synchronic analysis

The synchronic analysis of the Akkadian data should take into account all three forms of the feminine noun - unbound, bound, and construct - as well as the phonological rules of *a*-EPENTHESIS, *i*-ADDITION, VOWEL DELETION, and VOWEL SHORTENING, which were motivated and described above. First I present a sampling of forms, excluding only certain problematic ones which will be treated further on.

|     | *Unbound*   | *Bound*   | *Construct* | *Gloss*    |
|-----|-------------|-----------|-------------|------------|
| (a) | 'amtu       | 'amat-    | 'amat       | bondwoman  |
| (b) | tertu       | terta-    | terti       | order      |
| (c) | biltu       | bilat-    | bilat       | tribute    |
| (d) | 'aššatu[55] | 'aššat-   | 'aššat      | wife       |
| (e) | 'erṣetu     | 'erṣet-   | 'erṣet      | land       |
| (f) | šarratu     | šarrat-   | šarrat      | queen      |
| (g) | qištu       | qišta-    | qišti       | gift       |
| (h) | napištu     | napišta-  | napišti     | life       |
| (i) | tukultu[56] | tukulta-  | tukulti     | trust      |
| (j) | šeriktu     | šerikta-  | šerikti     | gift       |
| (k) | ṣibuutu     | ṣibut-    | ṣibut       | request    |
| (l) | ḫiteetu     | ḫitet-    | ḫitet       | loss       |
| (m) | maštiitu    | maštit-   | maštit      | drink      |
| (n) | narkabtu    | narkabta- | narkabti    | chariot    |
| (o) | šipirtu     | šipirta-  | šipirti     | work       |

## 7.5. Synchronic analysis

## 7.5.1. RULE 1 of FEMININE SUFFIX SELECTION

Upon even cursory inspection the data manifest clear patterns. Bound forms that have *at* are identical to their corresponding construct forms (cases a,c-f). Moreover, in these forms

[55] For the later development of this form to *'aštu/'altu*, see §7.6 below.

[56] For the poetic variant *tuklatu(m)* (e.g., Lambert BWL p. 88:290) see §7.7 below.

the unbound stems that end in two consonants (d-f) rather than one (a,c) have *at* (>*et*
where the stem vowel is *e*). Thus, only for stems of the type (a,c) are there two alternating forms, unbound with *t*, bound and construct with *at*. Clearly (a,c) belong to the same
group as (d-f). There is strong motivation, therefore, to posit unitary underlying representations for (a,c), e.g., /'am+at/ and /bil+at/ and to derive the unbound forms, with case
endings, *via* VOWEL DELETION:

| /'am+at+u/ | /bil+at+u/ | |
|---|---|---|
| ['amtu] | [biltu] | VOWEL DELETION |

VOWEL DELETION does not apply to forms (d-f).

It might be thought that in forms (a,c-f) the *a* of the suffix *at* is inserted not morphologically but phonologically. That is, perhaps *a* is inserted in bound and construct forms of
the type (a,c) and in all forms of (d-f) in order to break up an impermissible consonant
cluster, /-CC#/ or /-CCC-/. In other words, if the underlying representations of the stems
in cases (d-f) are of the shape /#CVCC/, the suffixation of /t/ would meet the structural
description of the Akkadian rule of *a*-EPENTHESIS (§ 3), which would insert *a* between
the second and third of three consecutive consonants. Perhaps, then, the second *a* in
*šarratu* (case f) is inserted by the same rule that inserts [a] in /libb+šu/ 'his heart' and
produces [libbašu]. This account may work for cases (d-f), but it does not work for the
bound and construct forms of cases (a,c). Moreover, with respect to (d-f), all other bound
and construct forms exhibit their underlying suffixes on the surface. The native Akkadian
speaker, knowing that there is a suffix /at/ in the language, would interpret [a] in a
feminine suffix as part of the morpheme, whether it originated morphologically or phonologically. From a synchronic standpoint, the *at* in cases (d-f) should be considered morphophonemic, like *at* in cases (a,c).

Let us assume an underlying representation of case (c) as /bil+t/. The rule of *a*-EPENTHE-
SIS would normally apply (cf. cases b,g-j,n,o):

| /bil+t+ka/ | 'your tribute' |
|---|---|
| [biltaka] | *a*-EPENTHESIS |

The rule produces an incorrect output. Likewise in the construct form, which underlyingly
would end in a double consonant. The *i*-ADDITION rule applies (cf. cases b,g-j,n,o):

| /bil+t/ | 'tribute of' |
|---|---|
| [bilti] | *i*-ADDITION |

Again the appropriate Akkadian rule produces an incorrect output.

Now we are confronted by two alternatives. We could invent an ad hoc rule of epenthesis
to apply to cases such as (a,c), or we could posit underlying suffixes of the shape /at/,
which requires no special rules or conditions. Clearly the latter approach is simpler and
preferable. Since the grammar of any Akkadian dialect must include a feminine suffix
/at/ at least for cases (a,c), it is simpler and more straightforward to posit /at/, rather

than /t/, in cases (d-f) as well. Even if *at* had originated as *t* with the preceding *a* inserted secondarily, surface *at* was certainly morphologized prior to the earliest attested Akkadian.

We can now formulate one rule governing the selection of /at/ or /t/ on the basis of cases (d-f):

> RULE 1:    Select /at/ when the underlying stem ends in /CC/.

It should be noted that this rule corresponds to rule (i) in §7.1 above and subsumes "patterns" 4 and 5 in Reiner (1966:119-120). Cases (a,c), however, are not covered by RULE 1. Their situation is complicated by the superficial identity of their stem shape, /(C)VC/, and that of forms (b) and (g) and will be discussed below.

### 7.5.2.  RULE 2 of FEMININE SUFFIX SELECTION

Another pattern that is clearly displayed by the data is that cases (b,g-o) show no *a* preceding the feminine *t*-suffix in any form. Synchronically, then, an underlying feminine morph /t/ must be posited for all of them. An examination of the bound and construct forms leads to a division of these cases into two groups, those which end in *t* in both the bound and construct forms (cases k-m) and those which end in *a* in the bound form and *i* in the construct form (cases b,g-j,n,o). But only /t/ is morphophonemic; *a* is inserted through *a*-EPENTHESIS and *i* is attached by *i*-ADDITION. Essentially, then, a division between cases (k-m) and (b,g-j,n,o) would be artificial on the underlying level. The stems in all these cases share the common structural property that they end in no more than one consonant (including, of course, no consonant at all, i.e., a vowel). We may now formulate a second rule governing the selection of /at/ or /t/:

> RULE 2:    Select /t/ when the underlying stem ends in /V(C)/.

RULE 2 subsumes patterns 1, 2, 3, and 6 in Reiner (1966:117-121).

### 7.5.3.  RULE 3 of FEMININE SUFFIX SELECTION

RULE 2 cannot stand by itself because it would include in its structural description cases (a,c), which take the suffix /at/. We must therefore modify RULE 2 or formulate another rule to cover cases (a,c). Since RULE 2 captures a phonological generalization that encompasses cases such as (k-m) as well as (b,g-j,n,o), we would not want to sacrifice it unnecessarily. We would do better to formulate a third rule to derive cases of the type (a,c).

It has been remarked above that stems such as we find in cases (a,c) are superficially identical to stems such as we find in cases (b,g). Yet cases (a,c) take the suffix /at/ while cases (b,g) take /t/. It is necessary to determine whether any factors can be identified that distinguish the two sets of forms in the grammar. There is a historical difference between the two sets that perhaps has a surviving reflex in the synchronic grammar. The stems of cases (a,c) have the reconstructed shape \*/CVC/, while the stems of cases (b,g) have the reconstructed shape \*/CVGVC/, where "G" represents a phonological glide; cf. \**ta'/war* 'command, order', \**qayiš* 'donate, give'. Perhaps we should then posit, with most grammars of Akkadian, underlying stems with long vowels, viz., /teer/, /qiiš/, etc. The native speaker might have associated such stems with the verbs with which they are etymologically related. These verbs are of the middle-weak class and themselves exhibit long vowels as the result of diachronic vowel-glide contraction; cf. the forms *qaašu* 'to give', *'iqiiš* 'he gave', *'iqaaš* 'he gives'. Positing long vowels in stems such as /teer/ and /qiiš/, however, assumes the existence of the long vowels as abstract representations (see Hyman 1970, Brame 1972), since VOWEL SHORTENING (§6) would most likely have eliminated the long vowel phonetically in all forms of the feminine noun.

We might have reason, then, to posit underlying stems /teer/ and /qiiš/ for cases (b,g). With the addition of the feminine morph /t/ the surface forms can be derived as follows:

|  |  |  |
|---|---|---|
| /teer+t/ | /qiiš+t/ | |
| [tert] | [qišt] | VOWEL SHORTENING |

In this way cases (b,g) can be distinguished from cases (a,c) underlyingly.

The assumption of underlying abstract long vowels in (b,g) is highly theoretical, however, and has little synchronic motivation. The historically long vowels in (b,g) would have been shortened diachronically and would never have appeared phonetically. These stems were then restructured to contain only short vowels, viz., /ter/ and /qiš/. Such stems historically took the suffix /t/ and not /at/.

It is therefore preferable to mark in the lexicon those stems of the shape /CVC/ that undergo RULE 3. For [$\pm$ Rule $x$] as a lexical feature, see Chomsky and Halle (1968), King (1969:135-136), Kisseberth (1970c:56-57), Schane (1973b:828), Kiparsky (1973a: 16-17). It would have been nice to include the historically long stem-vowels of cases (b,g) in the rules of FEMININE SUFFIX SELECTION, but we cannot attribute historical information to the child learning his or her language (cf. §1.4). The third rule of FEMININE SUFFIX SELECTION derives cases (a,c) and may be formulated as follows:

RULE 3: Select /at/ when the stem is /CVC/.

Clearly RULE 3 is more highly marked (its conditions are less general) than RULE 2 and should be ordered to precede it (Kiparsky 1973c, Hooper 1976:59). Whichever lexical stem does not undergo the more specialized RULE 3 undergoes RULE 2. Note that this solution resolves the contradiction between rules (ii) and (iv) in §7.1 above and incorporates the correct historical observation of rule (x) there.

7.5.3.1.    DIACHRONIC EXPLANATION OF RULE 3

The morphological rules 1 and 2 of FEMININE SUFFIX SELECTION are subordinate to the phonotactic constraint that disallows sequences of [CC] in one syllable. Zimmern (1890:372-373,378) also explained the principle governing the selection of /at/ or /t/ as one concerning sequences of consonants, but his principle involved tendencies to separate similarly articulated consonants, such as *kalbatu* 'bitch' in which *l* and *b* are permitted to be contiguous and *šalamtu* 'corpse' in which *l* and *m* are separated to facilitate articulation (contrast Brockelmann 1903a:6,n.1). Zimmern's principle is limited in scope and fails to apply to most cases, e.g., *tukultu*. The phonotactic constraint suffices to explain RULES

1 and 2, but it does not account for RULE 3. The suffixation of /at/ to monosyllabic stems originates in historical factors. For one, there was an apparent prehistoric development in Semitic in which biconsonantal bases were expanded morphologically to resemble triconsonantal forms (cf. already Nöldeke 1910:124ff.). Second, several originally initial-*w (perhaps denominative) stems took *at*, such as **wabilatu* > *bilatu* > *biltu* 'tribute'; **wašinatu* > *šinatu* > *šittu* 'sleep' (cf. Barth 1967 [1894]: §62e; Sarauw 1939:19-20). And third, final-weak stems suffixed *t*, as in **šanat* 'year', and only secondarily appeared to have the suffix *at* (cf. Barth 1887:604ff.). Because biconsonantal Akkadian stems take /at/ for historical reasons, it is necessary for the grammar to include a morphologically motivated rule such as RULE 3.

### 7.6. Counterexamples explained

Apart from the problem posed by certain stems that take either the suffix /at/ or /t/, which will be resolved in §7.7, there are a number of apparent counterexamples to the three rules of FEMININE SUFFIX SELECTION. Most of the synchronic exceptions to the rules can be traced to diachronic factors, and an examination of the exceptions actually confirms the existence of the rules as I have formulated them (§§7.51-7.53).

A case in point concerns the word *'ittu* 'omen' (data and references in Oppenheim et al. 1955- , vol. 7:304ff.). The historical base of the word is *'idat*. When case endings are added, the phonological rules produce ['ittu]:

| /'id+at+u/ | |
| --- | --- |
| 'idtu | VOWEL DELETION |
| ['ittu] | HOMORGANIC CONSONANT ASSIMILATION |
| | (see §7.1) |

The various dialects, however, attest two construct forms, *'idat* and *'itti*.[57] Clearly those dialects which have a construct form *'itti* (through the application of *i*-ADDITION) restructured the underlying stem of *'ittu* as /'it+t/. Such restructuring could only have occurred after */'id/ had lost its marking in the lexicon to undergo RULE 3.

A more complex situation obtains concerning such words as *beltu* 'lady' and *martu* 'daughter', which have the bound/construct forms *belet* and *marat*, respectively. The most straightforward manner of accounting for these forms synchronically is to posit underlying forms /bel+at/ and /mar+at/, implementing RULE 3. When case endings are suffixed, the VOWEL DELETION rule produces the correct surface output.

Historically, however, the underlying stems had long vowels, viz., */beel/ and */maar/. The former is derived from **ba'l* (cf. West Semitic) with contraction of *a* + pharyngeal

---

[57] Not *'itta-*, which is the bound form; correct Oppenheim et al. (1955-    , vol. 7:304b).

to *ee* (von Soden 1969:§ 24e; cf. Sarauw 1939:129-130). [58] The latter is derived from
*\*mar'* [59] with metathesis of *r* and *'* and contraction of *a* + laryngeal to *aa*; i.e., *\*mar'*
> *ma'r* > *maar* (cf. Gelb 1955:100b; Dahood et al. 1965:38; Malone 1971b: 412,n.66;
Hirsch 1972: 398; contrast von Soden 1969:§ § 15b,20d). We would therefore expect
*beltu* and *martu*, with historically long stem-vowels and masculine counterparts *beelu* and
*maaru*, to behave like cases (b,g), undergoing RULE 2 and forming bound forms through
*a*-EPENTHESIS (viz., *\*belta-* and *\*marta-*) and construct forms through *i*-ADDITION (viz.,
*\*belti* and *\*marti*). In fact, some varieties of Akkadian do treat *beltu* in this way and
form a construct *belti* (e.g., EA 20:9,25; Mitanni MB). But such cases are found typically
in peripheral areas, where Akkadian was not the native language.

It is true that in literary Akkadian (data and references in von Soden 1932:211) one
finds constructs such as *belti* (for *belet*), *marti* (for *marat*), and *šubti* (for *šubat*). These
words, however, are not simple constructs but archaic formations in which the genitive
case ending *i* is preserved word-finally. When one also regards masculine formations such
as *bulṭi* (for *buluṭ*) and *šigari* (for *šigar*), it becomes evident that these forms result from
the conservation of *i* on a base of the shape /CVCVC/ (cf. *šigari*). The rule of VOWEL
DELETION then reduced *\*beleti* to *belti* and *\*šubati* to *šubti* just as it reduced *\*buluṭi*
to *bulṭi*. Proof positive is the form *šigari* in which VOWEL DELETION is constrained by
the *r* (§ 5.511).

Normally *beltu* and *martu* behave instead as cases (a,c). This superficial anomaly may be
explained historically, however, by appealing to restructuring as a result of ("weak")
phonological change (see Kiparsky 1971a [1965]: esp. 3; King 1969:51). Originally the
bases *\*/ba'l/* and *\*/mar'/* met the structural description of RULE 1 and took the suffix
*/at/*. In fact, Old Assyrian conserves the stem *\*mar'* in the construct form *mer'at* (written
*me-er-a-at*; references in Hecker 1968b:§ 27c). [60] In Old Akkadian the forms *beelatum* and
*beeletum* are attested (references in Gelb 1957:90) showing the original *at* suffix on the
surface. In Old Assyrian the form *beelatum* is encountered; cf., e.g., *be-la-ti-šu* 'his lady'
(AOB I p. 26:2). However, already in OAkk. we begin to find the form *beltum* (references in Gelb 1957:90), while the construct remains *belet*. We must, accordingly, reconstruct a diachronic change of *\*beeletum* to *beltum* (cf. already Delitzsch 1906:§ 45a, who
posits this rule synchronically, however). This reconstructed change involves the shortening
of the stem-vowel and, as a consequence, elision of the suffix vowel when vocalic (i.e.,
case) endings are attached; or the shortening of the stem-vowel as a result of exceptional
elision of the suffix vowel and formation of a closed syllable. Such a phonological change
affected only a few, common words, such as *beltum* and *martum*, and is thus an example
of "weak" phonological change (see Malkiel 1968a:33ff., 1968b:29). One can hypothesize
that this limited innovation occurred through some phonetic factor such as allegro speech
(cf. Greenberg 1966:517) and had affected only frequently used vocabulary words (cf.

[58] For a discussion of the phonetic problems involved, see Blake (1945).

[59] Etymologically equivalent to Aramaic *mr'* 'master' (references in Jean and Hoftijzer 1965:166-167).

[60] For the extra vowel grapheme as an indicator of the laryngeal, cf. Sarauw (1939:51-52); Aro
(1953:3-4); Finet (1956:§ 3a); Reiner (1964:170, 1973:28); Ungnad and Matouš (1969:§ 14b); Greenstein and Marcus (1976:74).

Fidelholtz 1975). In any event, perhaps both forms *beelatum* and *beltum* coexisted for a time, as in OAkk.[61] But in the spoken language (for the literary language, see § 7.7) *beltu(m)* superseded *beeletum* in the unbound form while the bound and construct form *belet* (originally \**beelet*) continued in use. Speakers, knowing only the forms *beltu(m)* and *belet*, restructured the underlying form as /bel+at/ and derived correct phonetic realizations through the regular phonological rules.[62] Thus synchronically *beltu* would appear like cases (a,c) and would undergo RULE 3. I surmise that in Babylonian and in Assyrian from MA on the same historical process affected *martu*.

Now although the analysis I propose may seem at first blush to be a bit forced, a parallel and more radical development of "weak" phonological change and resultant restructuring is more transparent in the history of another Akkadian feminine noun, *'aššatu* 'wife' (case d). In the earlier dialects *'aššatu* behaves like any other word subject to FEMININE SUFFIX SELECTION RULE 1. However, sporadically in OB and Standard Babylonian, and regularly in NB, *'aššatu* becomes *'aštu* (> *'altu* in NB), with construct *'ašti* (> *'alti* in NB; data and references in Oppenheim et al. 1955- , vol.1/2:462-465, esp.465a). Clearly through some factor, perhaps articulation in allegro speech, geminate [šš] was reduced to single [š], thereby conditioning the elision of the suffix vowel [a] and producing unbound ['aštu] (> ['altu] in NB; cf. Brockelmann 1966 [1908]:71). The phenomenon occurs in other words, too (Ylvisaker 1912: § 9). The stem was then restructured as /'aš+t/, undergoing RULE 2, and the construct was formed by the phonological rule of *i*-ADDITION.

## 7.7. Alternant forms of 7.3 explained

We return to the problem of alternating forms, with ostensibly the same stem employing /at/ or /t/ (§ 7.3). Within the same *spoken* dialect such alternations are most rare. Thus *qaššatum* 'holiness' beside the more common *qadištum* noted by Reiner (1966:120) is a dialectal form in OB Mari (von Soden 1958-81:891b). Other alternations are *napšatu(m)* beside *napištu(m)* (OA *napaštum*; cf. Hecker 1968b: § § 8a,54a; von Soden 1958-81:736a),[63] *kabattu* beside *kabtatu*, *beeletu(m)* beside *beltu(m)* (cf. von Soden 1969: § 60b), *bukurtu* beside *bukratu* (e.g., Ebeling *Handerhebung* p.60:3), *mitratu* beside *mitirtu* (see Lambert 1969:250).

Typically in each of these pairs the form with morphophonemic /at/ rather than /t/ is restricted to poetic or literary texts, those written in "Hymnal-Epic Dialect" (the literary

---

[61] For the coexistence of older and innovative forms within the same dialect, see Weinreich, Labov and Herzog (1968:esp. 149); Malkiel (1968b:72); Labov (1972).

[62] Early comparative Semitic grammarians explained *beltu* as the result of analogy, presumably to forms like (b,g); e.g., Brockelmann (1903a:11). This explanation does not account for the conservation of the construct *belet* as opposed to *terti*, *qišti*, etc.

[63] The word *napaštum* also occurs in BIN 4, #9:16 *i-na-pá-áš-ti-kà* (= *'in(a) napaštiika*) 'by your life' (so Oppenheim et al. 1955- , vol. 2:144a); contrast Hecker (1968b: § 145b), who reads *'ina baštiika* 'in your strength'. Against Hecker's interpretation is that were his reading correct we would expect a spelling *i-ba-áš-ti-kà*, with the *n* of *'ina* assimilated to the next consonant after the intervening *a* was deleted; cf. *i-pì-kà-ma* (=*'ina piikaama*) 'by your word' (BIN 4, 10:15); *a-ba-aš-tí-ka* (=*'ana baštiika*) 'to your strength' (ibid.:25).

language of the OB period) and in Standard Babylonian (the literary language of the post-OB period). For example, compare *napištum* (CH prolog 3:66) beside *napšatam* (ibid. 4:2) in HED; *napištašu* (En. el. IV:17) beside *napšassu* ( = /napišat+su/; ibid.:18) in SB; *kabtassa* ( = /kabatat+sa/; Descent of Ishtar 96, Nineveh recension) beside *kabattašu* (loc. cit., Assur recension; Borger 1963:2.91). We are dealing with a matter of literary diction in which /at/ is selected for stems that would in spoken language take /t/, as observed by von Soden (1932:220ff.). The fact that poetic grammar often exercises rules not used in regular speech has been noted generally (cf. Kiparsky 1973b:238-239). In terms of the rules for FEMININE SUFFIX SELECTION, RULE 1 (or 3) is artificially applied to stems to which RULE 2 would apply otherwise. Reiner (1966:120) derives the alternant forms, such as *damiqtu* beside *damqatu* 'good', from different bases. But *damqatu*, a rare literary word (see Oppenheim et al. 1955-  , vol. 3:68ff.), can be derived more simply, as can all the above poetic variants, by implementing RULE 1 instead of RULE 2:

/damiq+at+u/

[damqatu]          VOWEL DELETION

One can only guess at the poets' reason for utilizing the /at/ suffix for literary forms. Perhaps they considered forms with *at* as more archaic since some forms with transparent *at*, such as *beeletu(m)*, are historically older than their counterparts in which underlying /at/ is opaque (see above). Or perhaps the poets sought to establish an artificial surface similarity in the singular:plural paradigm with singular *qatlatu*, plural *qatlaatu*. The singular forms would then constitute "back formations" from their plurals. Empirical support for this hypothesis may be adduced from singular and plural forms that have the same meaning, e.g., sing. *napištu* and *napšatu* 'life' and pl. *napšaatu* 'life' (data and references in von Soden 1958-81:738). Or perhaps metrical considerations played a role, yielding words ending in a trochaic accent (see § 5.411), e.g., *napšássu* for *napíštašu*. Whatever the motivation, poetic feminine formations in *at* instead of *t* are not exceptions to the rules but the results of manipulations of the rules, creating literary forms distinguishable from their vernacular counterparts.

## 8. RULES AND AKKADIAN SYLLABLE STRUCTURE

### 8.1. Restatement of the rules

As I indicated at the outset (§ 1.2), most of the rules I have studied above can be understood as expressions of the language's concern to eliminate poorly-formed syllables and to create properly-formed ones. These are the rules in their relevant aspects:

*a*-EPENTHESIS:   Insert the vowel *a* in the environment CC_C.

*i*-ADDITION:   Insert the vowel *i* in the environment CC_#

VOWEL DELETION:   Delete a vowel in the environment VC_CV.

VOWEL SHORTENING:  Delete a vowel segment in the context V_CC.

FEMININE SUFFIX SELECTION:  Select the suffix /at/ if the base ends
in CC; select /t/ elsewhere.

## 8.2.  The rules and the Akkadian syllable

In any standard grammatical theory, not to speak of grammatical studies in Akkadian, these rules would have to be described individually. This is so because each rule differs from the others either in the process that the rule prescribes or in the context in which the rule applies, or both. This is unfortunate, however, because even cursory analysis reveals that these rules share a basic property: they prevent the surface formation of overweight syllables, those containing more than three segments. The rules of *a*-EPENTHESIS, *i*-ADDITION, and FS SELECTION serve to prevent the surfacing of consonant clusters within a syllable; the rule of VOWEL SHORTENING reduces an overweight (*CVVC*) syllable to one of three segments; and the rule of VOWEL DELETION fails to apply in the event that it would produce either a syllable of four segments (*CVVC* or *CVCC*) or a consonant cluster within a syllable (*CCV*). Using the principles of syllabification delineated above in § 2, we may describe the typical output of the rules in the following sequences: *CVC$CV$CV* (*a*-EPENTHESIS), *CVC$CV* (*i*-ADDITION), *CVC$CV* (VOWEL SHORTENING), *CVC$CVC* or *CVC$CVC$CV* (FS SELECTION), *CVC$CV* (VOWEL DELETION). In other words, these rules produce sequences of syllables none of which is more complex than *CVC* and which clearly tend toward the widespread fundamental pattern *CV$CV*.... The phonological processes of *a*-EPENTHESIS, *i*-ADDITION, VOWEL SHORTENING, VOWEL DELETION, and the morphologically related rule of FS SELECTION operate on more complex syllabic structures in order to yield simpler, "preferred syllable structures" (Schane 1973b:822-828; 1973a:53,118-119; Kiparsky 1971b:604; Hyman 1975:161-164; for Semitic, O'Leary 1969:129-138; Fischer 1969). Akkadian does not tolerate syllables of more than three segments.

## 8.3.  The functional unity of the rules

We have seen that it is advantageous and of explanatory value to speak in terms of syllable structure. Most grammars of Semitic languages and those of Akkadian in particular speak only of consonant clusters in various positions (e.g., Reiner 1966:43-44; von Soden 1969:§7c; Moscati 1969:§9.14). As a consequence they miss an important generalization. Brockelmann (1966 [1908]:61-71) and others (e.g., Speiser 1967:375), however, recognized the pertinence of syllable structure in explaining impermissible consonant clusters in Semitic. These observations have been echoed in more recent times for Afroasiatic as a whole by Diakonoff (1965:25,29; cf. O'Leary 1969:26-27,129-138): "According to rules common to Semito-Hamitic, . . . no syllable can begin . . . with two consonants. Neither can a syllable end in two consonants." Our study, which incorporates VOWEL SHORTENING into the set of syllable-related rules, enables us to capture the more encompassing generalization that no syllable may contain more than three segments.

The rules of *a*-EPENTHESIS, *i*-ADDITION, VOWEL SHORTENING, VOWEL DELETION, and FS SELECTION, though dissimilar in form, serve a unitary function: to produce well-formed syllable structures. Compare the remarks of Kisseberth (1970a:293): "The unity of a set of rules may not rest upon the similarity of their structural descriptions, but rather upon the similarity of their function. Or to put the point in a slightly different way, rules may be alike in having a common effect . . . ." We may therefore follow Kisseberth (1969, 1970a, 1970b, 1972), Kiparsky (1972b:213-221; 1973a:57-86), and others (e.g., Sommerstein 1974; Pyle 1974; Hooper 1976:221ff.) and describe a set of rules such as these in Akkadian as a "conspiracy" of rules. Observe that this conspiracy includes not only rules of phonology but also a rule of morphology, that of FEMININE SUFFIX SELECTION. The participation of morphological rules in a phonological conspiracy has been noted elsewhere, too (e.g., Kiparsky 1972b:220; 1973a:77; cf. Cook 1971). Typically phonological conspiracies serve to prevent the formation of surface configurations that contravene a phonotactic constraint of the language (cf. also Shibatani 1973; Clayton 1976; Goyvaerts 1978:101-118). Kiparsky (1972b:217) goes even further in drawing universal implications: "it seems to be true that phonological conspiracies always function to avert configurations which must be characterized as complex or highly marked, in terms of universal grammar." [64] The effect of the Akkadian conspiracy is to reduce complex syllabic structures to more common shapes and therefore supports Kiparsky's surmise.

## 8.4. The phonotactic constraint on Akkadian syllable structure

It is evident from the conspiratorial set of rules that Akkadian possessed a phonotactic constraint prohibiting the formation of complex syllable types. But it is not evident how to describe the relationship between this phonotactic constraint and each of the five rules. Negatively, the constraint blocks the application of VOWEL DELETION in certain environments. Positively, the constraint may be said to instigate the conspiracy comprising of *a*-EPENTHESIS, *i*-ADDITION, VOWEL SHORTENING, and FEMININE SUFFIX SELECTION. Or, positively again, VOWEL DELETION produces more complex syllables, but permissible ones. Negatively, the other four rules conspire to block the formation of impermissible syllables. Because the rules more often promote proper syllable structure rather than restrict the application of VOWEL DELETION, it is best to follow Kisseberth (1972:217) and describe the constraint as a positive device. Because Kisseberth did not understand conspiracies such as the one in Akkadian with reference to syllable structure, he offered a formulation such as this: PRECEDING OR FOLLOWING TWO CONSONANTS, THERE MUST BE A SYLLABIC SEGMENT (= a vowel in Semitic). In terms of the Akkadian conspiracy, *a*-EPENTHESIS and *i*-ADDITION function to insert a vowel where the constraint requires

---

[64] Kiparsky does not explain conspiracies with regard to "derivational constraints" (constraints that can block a process at any point in a derivation from the morphophonemic level to the phonetic), as Kisseberth does. He argues that conspiratorial rules all lead to linguistic simplicity in making rules more transparent; i.e., the output of a rule clearly manifests the prior application of the rule (Kiparsky 1973a: 75-82). In Akkadian, e.g., the constraint against the deletion of the epenthetic *a* in *libbašu* 'his heart' would function to preserve the *a* that manifests the rule of *a*-EPENTHESIS. Kiparsky's explanation, though, does not explain the rise of the *a*-EPENTHESIS rule in the first place. Kisseberth's reference to derivational constraints does. I discuss the relevance of derivational constraint in the Akkadian conspiracy at greater length in Greenstein (1977:127-131).

it; VOWEL SHORTENING functions to delete a segment where the constraint requires it; FEMININE SUFFIX SELECTION functions to uphold the constraint morphologically; and VOWEL DELETION functions freely except in the event that it would violate the constraint, i.e., VOWEL DELETION upholds the constraint.

By including VOWEL SHORTENING, a rule which exists in languages other than Semitic, such as Yawelmani (Kenstowicz and Kisseberth 1979:83-85), which, like Akkadian, possesses rules that resolve consonant clusters, too, we may broaden the definition to embody a constraint on syllable structure (cf. Schane 1973a:53,118-119; Hooper 1976:192-193,221ff.). This constraint has three parts:

(1) Every syllable must begin with a consonant.

(2) No syllable may contain two contiguous consonants.

(3) No syllable (except perhaps in word-final position) may contain more than three segments.

The Akkadian rules of phonology and morphology serve to satisfy these constraints.


## 8.5. Reformulation of the rules in terms of syllable structure

We must now reformulate the rules in the Akkadian conspiracy in terms of syllable structure. Since the rules are all subject to, or agents of, the constraint, information in the rules that duplicates information already contained within the constraint is redundant and should be discarded (cf. Kisseberth 1970a:304-305; Kiparsky 1972b:217). It is a truism that the rules that simplify syllable structures only operate when a complex syllable has been formed morphophonemically. But it is essential to bear in mind that underlying strings are also subject to syllabification. Thus the rules apply not simply to strings of consonants and vowels but to well-formed and malformed syllables. When morphemes are combined and recombined, the segments are likely to be rearranged into different syllable structures, well-formed and poorly-formed. Poorly-formed syllables are those that violate the constraint and will be reformed according to one of the conspiratorial rules (cf. Goyvaerts 1978:109).


### 8.5.1. Reformulation of *a*-EPENTHESIS

The rule of *a*-EPENTHESIS was formulated above in terms of a sequence of three consonants. This is no longer necessary. Since according to our understanding of Akkadian morphophonemics no more than three consonants can occur in an underlying sequence, the first of the three consonants will be syllabified with the preceding vowel (cf. § 2). For example, in /libb+šunu/ 'their heart' the first *b* will be assigned to the first syllable, *lib*, as *CVC* is an acceptable syllable structure. The second *b* is followed by a consonant, yielding a poorly-formed syllable of the shape *CCV*, viz., *bšu*. The only essential information in this case is that there is an underlying syllable containing the sequence *CC* in syllable-initial position, which violates part (2) of the constraint (§8.4). In such a case the vowel *a* is inserted between them to create a new syllable of the type *CV*, viz., *ba*. We may now reformulate *a*-EPENTHESIS as follows:

If a syllable begins with two consecutive consonants, insert *a* between them.

### 8.5.2. Reformulation of *i*-ADDITION

In a similar fashion we can revise the rule of *i*-ADDITION. The rule applies to two successive consonants at the end of a word. For example, in /libb#/ the first *b* belongs to the syllable *lib*, as in the above case of *a*-EPENTHESIS. The presence of the second *b* creates a syllable containing two contiguous consonants in syllable-final position, violating part (2) of the constraint. The addition of *i* creates a second syllable, *bi*, thereby alleviating the overweight first syllable. We may now formulate the rule of *i*-ADDITION as follows:

If a syllable ends in two contiguous consonants, add *i*.

It is noteworthy that there appear to be functional phonological reasons for resolving the syllable-final consonant cluster through *i*-ADDITION rather than through *a*-EPENTHESIS, which would also have done the trick. Were *a*-EPENTHESIS employed, two phonological processes rather than one would be required in most cases. For example, /tukul+t/ 'trust' forms its construct through *i*-ADDITION: *tukulti*. Were *a*-EPENTHESIS to apply, the derivation would require an additional process of VOWEL DELETION:

/tukul+t/

tukulat            \**a*-EPENTHESIS

\*[tuklat]          \*VOWEL DELETION

It is more economical to employ *i*-ADDITION.

Another consideration is that both in paradigmatic change and in the reordering of rules, the following principle is generally obeyed: "ALLOMORPHY TENDS TO BE MINIMIZED . . ." (Kiparsky 1971b:596ff., 612ff.; 1972b:208-209; King 1969:88; Hooper 1974:160). It has also been pointed out that the less the allomorphic variation, the greater the learnability of the underlying representation (Schane 1972:esp. 223-225; cf. Kaye 1975). With respect to *a*-EPENTHESIS, were it to apply to any form such as /libb#/, a surface allomorphy would emerge, viz., *libbu* 'heart' but construct \**libab* 'heart of', in which the underlying form /libb/ is transparent in the first instance but more opaque in the second. Through the process of *i*-ADDITION the construct form becomes *libbi*, and the underlying form /libb/ is transparent in both instances. Note that the same consideration pertains to the case of *tukultu* with its construct *tukulti*, as described above.

Yet a third consideration is the principle of Kenstowicz and Pyle (1973:27 et passim), which maintains that "All other things being equal, a rule which splits up a geminate cluster is less highly valued than a rule which must be constrained from doing so." For stems that contain a geminate cluster, such as /libb/, the *a*-EPENTHESIS rule would violate the empirically determined principle of Kenstowicz and Pyle by splitting the cluster, i.e., /libb/ → \**libab*, while *i*-ADDITION leaves the cluster intact. The behavior of Akkadian in this matter helps confirm the correctness of Kenstowicz and Pyle's principle.

### 8.5.3. Reformulation of VOWEL DELETION

The VOWEL DELETION rule can also be formulated in terms of the syllable structure constraint. Interestingly enough, this rule has frequently been formulated in standard grammatical studies of Akkadian in terms of syllables. Thus, Poebel (1939:48) spoke of the "elision of a short vowel in an open syllable immediately after a stressed open and short syllable," and Goetze (1947c:240) stated that Akkadian "does not tolerate the sequence of two short medial syllables and eliminates it by syncopating the second short vowel" (cf. Goetze 1946b:233; von Soden 1969:§12a; Kaufman 1974:26,n.70). Vowel deletion or reduction has also been expressed for other Semitic languages in terms of syllable sequences (e.g., Cantineau 1932; Bravmann 1977 [1953]:140; Malone 1969:549; 1975:7). However, the formulations for Akkadian contain much redundant information. Hirsch (1975:277) has already noticed a redundancy in the standard description of VOWEL DELETION as presented in von Soden (1969:§12a). This formulation singles out the vowel in the second syllable for deletion. But the first vowel could not be deleted in any event because it would produce a syllable-initial consonant cluster. For example, if the first vowel in /šupur+am/ 'send to me' were deleted, the resultant form *špuram would contain such a cluster. Akkadian VOWEL DELETION may be expressed most simply as follows:

> Delete the first vowel in a word (with the limitations and dialectal variations set forth in § 5.5).

All other environmental restrictions are already present in the syllable structure constraint and need not be re-stated.

The incorporation of VOWEL DELETION into Akkadian phonology semmingly poses a paradox. On the one hand the language possesses a constraint on syllable structure that places a premium on vowels, which break up consonant clusters and create well-formed syllables. On the other the language adopts VOWEL DELETION, a rule which threatens to collapse well-formed syllables into impermissible ones and must be prevented from applying in those contexts where it would produce malformed syllables. In this case, however, Akkadian seems not to have developed VOWEL DELETION out of its own instincts, as it were, as it does in a sense run against the grain of the phonology. Rather, VOWEL DELETION arose in Akkadian through the pressures of Sumerian, a non-Semitic language (§ 5.7). Again (see also §§7.2, 7.6), a somewhat odd synchronic phenomenon emerges out of historical circumstances.

### 8.5.4. Reformulation of VOWEL SHORTENING

The rule of VOWEL SHORTENING can likewise be simplified in terms of syllable structure as follows:

> Shorten a vowel that is not followed by a syllable boundary.

This rule obviously satisfies part (3) of the constraint and depends on it for its motivation.

### 8.5.5. Reformulation of FEMININE SUFFIX SELECTION

Similarly, the rules for FEMININE SUFFIX SELECTION (with the exception of the specially marked RULE 3) can be expressed:

> If the final syllable of a base ends in a consonant cluster, add /at/;
> add /t/ elsewhere.

There will be occasions on which the suffixation of /t/ will lead to the formation of a malformed syllable of the shape *CVVC*. Then the rule of VOWEL SHORTENING applies and derives correct forms, e.g.:

| | |
|---|---|
| /batuul/ | 'young man' |
| /batuul+t/ | FS SELECTION: 'young lady' |
| /batuul+t+u/ | CASE AFFIXATION |
| [batultu] | VOWEL SHORTENING |

In considering the conditions for FEMININE SUFFIX SELECTION in this way, we may draw possible implications for "Proto-Semitic." We have noted (following Brockelmann and others) that the Akkadian constraints on syllable structure appear to be common in Semitic. Therefore, it can be inferred that if Akkadian required two allomorphs, /at/ and /t/, for the feminine suffix, Proto-Semitic began to require two allomorphs – or some other epenthetic device – at the stage at which it came to assume the constraints on syllable structure.

### 8.6. Conclusions concerning the syllable in Akkadian phonology

Our studies indicate that Akkadian possessed a tripartite constraint on syllable structure virtually identical to that evidenced in West Semitic and, accordingly, characteristic of Semitic as a whole:

(a) The syllable must begin with a consonant.

(b) No syllable may contain two contiguous consonants.

(c) No syllable (except perhaps in word-final position) may contain more than three segments.

This constraint requires the rules of *a*-EPENTHESIS, *i*-ADDITION, VOWEL SHORTENING, FEMININE SUFFIX SELECTION, and the limitations on VOWEL DELETION to enforce it. As we have seen, the significance of these rules can be appreciated when they are viewed with regard to syllable structure. It should also be noted that the Assyrian rule of VOWEL HARMONY (n. 48 above) is sensitive to syllable patterning. The segment that undergoes VOWEL HARMONY must be in a light (two-segment) syllable and that syllable must be the penultimate in the word.

It should not be taken for granted that in each of the processes by which Akkadian brings its syllables into line with the constraint, a vowel segment is added or deleted.

Consonants are never deleted. A number of languages resolve a word-final consonant cluster by deleting the first (e.g., Sanskrit, French) or second (e.g., Finnish) member of the cluster (cf. Schane et al. 1974/75; de Chene and Anderson 1979:526). Japanese has a constraint against consonant clusters within syllables, just as Akkadian does. Yet, a recent experiment confirms that when speakers of Japanese are asked to reproduce a foreign word containing a cluster within a syllable, most will delete one of the consonants in their pronunciation (Greenberg 1981). Perhaps Akkadian forms proper syllables by vocalic operations only because in the structure of Semitic language the basic meaning of a lexical stem is borne by a scheme of consonants, the "root." Akkadian phonology would then be subordinate not only to a constraint on syllable structure but also to a functional concern to preserve the integrity of the root (cf. also § 8.5.2).

As a final observation, I would repeat that the above analysis of an important set of rules within Akkadian morphophonology lends further support to the existence of rule ordering (§ 5.5312) and directionality in rule application (§ 5.5313) and militates against non-transformational theories of phonology (e.g., Hudson 1980).

## REFERENCES

Ambros, Arne A.
 1969    "Zur Bedeutungsgeschichte der arabischen Nominalfrom fa"āl(at)." *WZKM* 62: 87-104.
Andersen, Henning
 1973    "Abductive and Deductive Change." *Lang* 49: 265-293.
Anderson, James M.
 1973    *Structural Aspects of Language Change.* London: Longman.
Aristar, A. M. R.
 1979    "The IIwy Verbs and the Vowel System of Proto-West Semitic." *AAL* 6: 209-225.
Aro, Jussi
 1953    "Abnormal Plene Writings in Akkadian Texts." *St. Or.* 19/11. Helsinki: Societas Orientalis Fennica.
 1955    "Studien zur mittelbabylonischen Grammatik." *St. Or.* 20. Helsinki: Societas Orientalis Fennica.
 1965    "Parallels to the Akkadian Stative in the West Semitic Languages." pp. 407-411. In *Studies in Honor of B. Landsberger on His Seventy-Fifth Birthday = AS* 16. Chicago: Oriental Institute.
 1971    Review of *Briefe aus der Leidener Sammlung* by R. Frankena and of *Briefe aus dem Archive des Šamaš-Ḫāzir* by F. R. Kraus. *OLZ* 66: 245-252.
Barth, Jakob
 1887    "Vergleichende Studien." *ZDMG* 41: 603-641.
 1967    [1894] *Die Nominalbildung in den semitischen Sprachen.* Hildesheim: Ohms.
 1903a.   Review of *Die Femininendung* t *im semitischen Sprachen* by C. Brockelmann. *ZDMG* 57: 628-636.
 1903b.   "Zu Brockelmann's Erwiderung." *ZDMG* 57: 798-804.
Bell, Alan and Hooper, Joan B.
 1978    "Issues and Evidence in Syllabic Phonology." pp. 3-22. In Bell and Hooper, eds. *Syllables and Segments.* Amsterdam/New York: North-Holland.

Ben-Hayyim, Z.
   1979    "Mono- and Bi-syllabic Middle Guttural Nouns in Samaritan Hebrew." *ANES* 11: 19-29.
Berkooz, Moshé
   1966    [1937] *The Nuzi Dialect of Akkadian: Orthography and Phonology*. New York: Kraus.
Blake, Frank R.
   1945    "Studies in Semitic Grammar III." *JAOS* 65: 111-116.
Blau, Joshua
   1977    "Marginalia Semitica III." *Israel Oriental Studies* 7: 14-31.
Blumstein, Sheila E.
   1978    "Segment Structure and the Syllable in   Aphasia." pp. 189-200. In A. Bell and J. B.
           Hooper, eds. *Syllables and Segments*.  Amsterdam/New York: North-Holland.
Böhl, F. M. Th. de Liagre
   1960    "La métrique de l'épopee babylonienne." pp. 145-152. In Paul Garelli, ed. *Gilgameš et sa
           légende*. Paris: Librairie C. Klincksieck.
Borger, Rykele
   1957    "niṣirti bārûti, Geheimlehre der Haruspizin." *Bi. Or.* 14: 190-195.
   1963    *Babylonische-assyrische Lesestücke*. 3 vols. Rome: Pontifical Biblical Institute.
Brame, Michael K.
   1972    "On the Abstractness of Phonology: Maltese ' ." pp. 22-61. In Brame, ed. *Contributions
           to Generative Phonology*. Austin: U. of Texas.
Bravmann, M. M.
   1977    *Studies in Semitic Philology*. Leiden: E. J. Brill.
Brockelmann, Carl.
   1903a.  "Die Femininendung *t* in Semitischen." *Schlesische Gesellschaft für vaterländische Kultur
           Jahresbericht* 81/4: 3-16.
   1903b.  "Gegen J. Barth, oben S. 628ff." *ZDMG* 57: 795-797.
   1966    [1908] *Grundriss der vergleichenden Grammatik der semitischen Sprachen I: Laut- und
           Formenlehre*. Hildesheim: Ohms.
Broselow, Ellen
   1979    "Cairene Arabic Syllable Structure." *Linguistic Analysis* 5: 345-382.
Buccellati, Giorgio
   1968    "An Interpretation of the Akkadian Stative as a Nominal Sentence." *JNES* 27: 1-12.
   1971    Review of *Phonétique comparée des dialects moyens-babyloniens du nord et de l'ouest*
           by G. Jucquois. *Oriens Antiquus* 10: 79-83.
Cantineau, Jean
   1932    "Elimination des syllables brèves en hébreu et en araméen biblique." *Bulletin d'études
           orientales* 2: 125-144.
Castellino, G. R.
   1962    *The Akkadian Personal Pronouns and Verbal System in the Light of Semitic and Hamitic*.
           Leiden: E. J. Brill.
Cena, R. M.
   1978    "When Is a Phonological Generalization Psychologically Real?" Bloomington: Indiana U.
           Linguistics Club.
Chafe, Wallace L.
   1968    "The Ordering of Phonological Rules." *International Journal of American Linguistics*
           34: 115-136.
   1970    *Meaning and Structure in Language*. Chicago: Chicago U.
Chambers, J. K. and Trudgill, Peter
   1980    *Dialectology*. Cambridge: Cambridge U.
Chapman, Raymond
   1973    *Linguistics and Literature*. Totown, NJ: Littlefield, Adams.

Chatman, Seymour
 1965    *A Theory of Meter*. Janua Linguarum, Series Minor 36. The Hague: Mouton.
Chen, Matthew Y. and Wang, William S.-Y.
 1975    "Sound Change: Actuation and Implementation." *Lang.* 51: 255-281.
de Chene, Brent and Anderson, Stephen R.
 1979    "Compensatory Lengthening." *Lang.* 55: 505-535.
Chomsky, Noam
 1977    *Essays on Form and Interpretation*. Amsterdam/New York: North-Holland.
Chomsky, Noam and Halle, Morris
 1968    *The Sound Pattern of English*. New York: Harper and Row.
Ciardi, John
 1959    *How Does a Poem Mean?* Boston: Houghton Mifflin.
Clayton, Mary L.
 1976    "The Redundance of Underlying Morpheme-Structure Conditions." *Lang.*  52: 295-313.
Cohen, David
 1970    *Etudes de linguistique sémitique et arabe*. Janua Linguarum, Series Practica 81. The Hague:
          Mouton.
Cook, Eung-Do
 1971    "Phonological Constraint and Syntactic Rule." *LI* 2: 465-478.
Dahood, M., Deller, K., and Köbert, R.
 1965    "Comparative Semitics: Some Remarks on a Recent Publication." *Or.* 34: 35-44.
Darwin, C. J.
 1976    "The Perception of Speech." pp. 175-226. In Edward C. Carterette and Morton P.
          Friedman, eds. *Handbook of Perception, Volume VII: Language and Speech*. New York:
          Academic.
Delitzsch, Friedrich
 1906    *Assyrische Grammatik*. 2nd. rev. ed. Berlin: Reuther and Reichard.
Deller, Karlheinz
 1958    Review of *L'accadien des lettres de Mari* by A. Finet. *WZKM* 55: 161-163.
 1959    "Lautlehre des Neuassyrischen." U. of Vienna: Ph.D. dissertation.
 1962a.  "Studien zur neuassyrischen Orthographie." *Or.* 31: 186-196.
 1962b.  "Zweisilbige Lautwerte des Typs KVKV im Neuassyrischen." *Or.* 31: 7-26.
 1965    Review of *Grammatik des Akkadischen*[4] by Ungnad and Matouš. *Or.* 34: 77-79.
 1969    "Die Briefe des Adad-šumu-uṣur." pp. 45-64. In *lišān mithurti = AOAT* 1. Neukirchen-Vluyn:
          Butzon and Bercker.
Diakonoff, I. M.
 1965    *Semito-Hamitic Languages: An Essay in Classification*. Moscow: Akademiia Nauk SSSR.
Donegan, Patricia J. and Stampe, David
 1978    "The Syllable in Phonology and Prosodic Structure." pp. 25-34. In Bell and Hooper, eds.
          *Syllables and Segments*. Amsterdam/New York: North-Holland.
Edzard, Dietz Otto
 1969    Review of *A Linguistic Analysis of Akkadian* by E. Reiner. *Bi. Or.* 26: 81b-84b.
 1973    "Die Modi beim älteren akkadischen Verbum." *Or.* 42: 121-141.
Eilers, Wilhelm
 1935    "Zur akkadischen Nominalbildung." *ZDMG* 89: 16*-19*.
Falkenstein, Adam
 1960    "Kontakte zwischen Sumerern und Akkadern auf sprachlichern Gebiet." *Genava* 8: 301-314.
 1964    *Das Sumerische*. Handbuch der Orientalisk. Leiden: E. J. Brill.
Fidelholtz, James L.
 1975    "Word Frequency and Vowel Reduction in English." pp. 200-213. In Robin E. Grossman
          et al., eds. *Papers from the Eleventh Regional Meeting*. Chicago Linguistic Society.

Finet, André
    1956    *L'accadien des lettres de Mari.* Brussels: Palais des Academies.
Fischer, W.
    1969    "Probleme der Silbenstruktur im Arabischen." pp. 65-69. In *Proceedings of the International Conference on Semitic Studies.* Jerusalem: Israel Academy of Sciences and Humanities.
Fodor, J. A., Bever, T. G., and Garrett, M. F.
    1974    *The Psychology of Language.* New York: McGraw-Hill.
Fronzaroli, Pelio
    1955    *La fonetica ugaritica.* Sussidi Eruditi 7. Rome: Edizioni di storia e letteratura.
Fujimura, Osamu and Lovins, Julie B.
    1978    "Syllables as Concatenative Phonetic Units." pp. 107-120. In Bell and Hooper, eds. *Syllables and Segments.* Amsterdam/New York: North-Holland.
Gelb, I. J.
    1955    "Notes on von Soden's Grammar." *Bi. Or.* 12: 93-111.
    1957    *A Glossary of Old Akkadian. MAD* 3. Chicago: Oriental Institute.
    1961a.   *Old Akkadian Writing and Grammar. MAD* 2 rev. ed. Chicago: Oriental Institute.
    1961b.   "WA = *aw, iw, uw* in Cuneiform Writing." *JNES* 20: 194-196.
    1963    *A Study of Writing.* rev. ed. Chicago: Chicago U.
    1965    "The Origin of the West Semitic *Qatala* Morpheme." pp. 72-80. In Stanisław Drewniak, ed. *Symbolae Linguisticae in honorem Georgii Kuryłowicz.* Wrocław: Polska Akademia Nauk.
    1969    *Sequential Reconstruction of Proto-Akkadian. AS* 18. Chicago: Oriental Institute.
    1970    "A Note on Morphographemics." pp. 73-77. In D. Cohen, ed. *Mélanges Marcel Cohen.* Janua Linguarum, Series Maior 27. The Hague: Mouton.
Goetze, Albrecht
    1942    "The So-Called Intensive of the Semitic Languages." *JAOS* 62: 1-8.
    1946a.   "Number Idioms in Old Babylonian." *JNES* 5: 185-202.
    1946b.   "Sequence of Two Short Syllables in Akkadian." *Or.* 15: 233-238.
    1947a.   Review of *The So-Called Relative Clauses in Accadian or the Accadian Particle ša* by O. E. Ravn. *JCS* 1: 73-80.
    1947b.   "The Akkadian Passive." *JCS* 1: 50-59.
    1947c.   "Short or Long *a*?" *Or.* 16: 239-250.
    1948    "Thirty Tablets from the Reigns of Abī-ešuḫ and Ammī-ditānā." *JCS* 2: 73-112.
Gordon, Cyrus H.
    1938    "The Dialect of the Nuzu Tablets." *Or.* 7: 32-63, 215-232.
Goshen-Gottstein, M. H.
    1964    "Semitic Morphological Structures: The Basic Morphological Structure of Biblical Hebrew." pp. 104-116. In *Studies in Egyptology and Linguistics in Honour of H. J. Polotsky.* Jerusalem: Israel Exploration Society.
Goyvaerts, Didier L.
    1978    *Aspects of Post-SPE Phonology.* Ghent/Antwerp: E. Story-Scientia.
Gragg, Gene B.
    1973    *Sumerian Dimensional Infixes. AOAT* Sonderreihe. Kevelaer/Neukirchen-Vluyn: Butzon and Bercker/Neukirchener Verlag.
Gray, Louis H.
    1934    *Introduction to Semitic Comparative Linguistics.* New York: Columbia University.
Greenberg, Cindy
    1981    "Syllable Structure in Second Language Acquisition." Unpublished paper presented at the annual meeting of the American Association for Applied Linguistics.
Greenberg, Joseph H.
    1960    "An Afro-Asiatic Pattern of Gender and Number Agreement" *JAOS* 80: 317-321.
    1966    "Synchronic and Diachronic Universals in Phonology." *Lang.* 42: 508-517.

1979     "Rethinking Linguistics Diachronically." *Lang.* 55: 275-290.

Greenstein, Edward L.

1976     "A Phoenician Inscription in Ugaritic Script?" *ANES* 8: 49-57.

1977     "Phonological Studies in Akkadian." Columbia U.: Ph.D. dissertation.

1980     "The Assimilation of Dentals and Sibilants with Pronominal š in Akkadian." *ANES* 12: 51-64.

Greenstein, Edward L. and Marcus, David.

1976     "The Akkadian Inscription of Idrimi." *ANES* 8: 59-96.

Grundt, Alice Wyland

1976     "Compensation in Phonology: Open Syllable Lengthening." Bloomington: Indiana U. Linguistics Club.

Gurney, O. R.

1954-56 "The Text of Enûma Eliš. New Additions and Variants." *AfO* 17: 353-356.

Haiman, John

1977     "Reinterpretation." *Lang.* 53: 312-328.

Haldar, Alfred

1963     "The Akkadian Verbal System." *Or.* 32: 246-279.

Halle, Morris

1964     "Phonology in Generative Grammar." pp. 334-352. In J. A. Fodor and J. J. Katz, eds. *The Structure of Language: Readings in the Philosophy of Language.* Englewood Cliffs: Prentice-Hall.

Halle, Morris and Keyser, Samuel Jay

1966     "Chaucer and the Study of Prosody." *College English* 28: 187-219.

Harms, Robert T.

1968     *Introduction to Phonological Theory.* Englewood Cliffs: Prentice-Hall.

Hecker, Karl

1968a.   Review of *A Linguistic Analysis of Akkadian* by E. Reiner. *ZDMG* 118: 157-162.

1968b.   *Grammatik der Kültepe-Texte. An. Or.* 44. Rome: Pontifical Biblical Institute.

1974     *Untersuchungen zur akkadischen Epik. AOAT* Sonderreihe 8. Neukirchen-Vluyn: Butzon and Bercker.

Heidel, Alexander

1940     *The System of the Quadriliteral Verb in Akkadian. AS* 13. Chicago: Oriental Institute.

Held, Moshe

1959     "*mhs/*mhš* in Ugaritic and Other Semitic Languages." *JAOS* 79: 169-176.

1961     "A Faithful Lover in an Old Babylonian Dialogue." *JCS* 15: 1-26.

1976     "Two Philological Notes on Enûma Eliš." pp. 231-239. In Barry L. Eichler et al., eds. *Kramer Anniversary Volume. AOAT* 25. Neukirchen-Vluyn: Butzon and Bercker.

Hetzron, Robert

1969     "The Evidence for Perfect *\*Y'AQTUL* and Jussive *\*YAQT'UL* in Proto-Semitic." *JSS* 14: 1-21.

1974     "Extrinsic Ordering in Classical Arabic." *AAL* 1/3: 1-20.

Hirsch, Hans

1967     Review of *Grammatik des Akkadischen* by Ungnad and Matouš. *ZA* 58: 324-327.

1972     "Zum Altassyrischen." *Or.* 41: 390-431.

1975     "Akkadische Grammatik - Erörterungen und Frägen." *Or.* 44: 245-322.

Hodge, Carlton T.

1975     "The Nominal Sentence in Semitic." *AAL* 2/4: 1-7.

Hooper, Joan G.

1972     "The Syllable in Phonological Theory." *Lang.* 48: 525-540.

1974     "Rule Morphologization in Natural Generative Phonology." pp. 160-170. In Anthony Bruck et al., eds. *Papers from the Parasession on Natural Phonology.* Chicago: Chicago Linguistic Society.

1976    *An Introduction to Natural Generative Phonology*. New York: Academic.
Hudson, Grover
1980    "Alternation in Non-Transformational Phonology." *Lang.* 56: 94-125.
Huizinga, Abel H.
1891    *Analogy in the Semitic Languages*. Baltimore: Johns Hopkins U.
Hyman, Larry M.
1970    "How Concrete Is Phonology?" *Lang.* 46: 58-76.
1975    *Phonology: Theory and Analysis*. New York: Holt, Rinehart and Winston.
1977    "On the Nature of Linguistic Stress." pp. 37-82. In Hyman, ed. *Studies in Stress and Accent*. Los Angeles: U. of Southern California.
Ingram, David
1978    "The Role of the Syllable in Phonological Development." pp. 143-155. In Bell and Hooper, eds. *Syllables and Segments*. Amsterdam/New York: North-Holland.
Ingria, Robert
1980    "Compensatory Lengthening as a Metrical Phenomenon." *LI* 11: 465-495.
Iverson, Gregory K. and Sanders, Gerald A.
1978    "The Functional Determination of Phonological Rule Interactions." Bloomington: Indiana U. Linguistics Club.
Jakobson, Roman
1962    "Typological Studies and Their Contribution to Historical Comparative Linguistics." pp. 523-532. In *Selected Writings I: Phonological Studies*. The Hague: Mouton.
1968    *Child Language, Aphasia, and Phonological Universals*. Janua Linguarum, Series Minor 72. The Hague: Mouton.
Jakobson, Roman and Halle, Morris
1957    "Phonology in Relation to Phonetics." pp. 215-231. In Louise Kaiser, ed. *Manual of Phonetics*. Amsterdam: North-Holland.
Jakobson, Roman and Waugh, Linda
1979    *The Sound Shape of Language*. Bloomington: Indiana U.
Janssens, G.
1975    "The Semitic Verbal Tense System." *AAL* 2/4: 9-14.
1975/76 "The Feminine Ending -(a)t in Semitic." *Orientalia Lovaniensia Periodica* 6/7: 277-284.
Jean, Charles-F. and Hoftijzer, Jacob
1965    *Dictionnaire des inscriptions sémitiques de l'ouest*. Leiden: E. J. Brill.
Jeffers, Robert J. and Lehiste, Ilse
1979    *Principles and Methods for Historical Linguistics*. Cambridge: MIT.
Jensen, John T.
1978    Review of *An Introduction to Natural Generative Phonology* by J. B. Hooper. *Lang.* 54: 667-674.
Johnstone, T. M.
1975    "The Modern South Arabian Languages." *AAL* 1/5: 1-29.
Jucquois, Guy
1966    *Phonétique comparée des dialects moyen-babyloniennes du nord et de l'ouest*. Louvain: Publications universitaires.
Kahn, Daniel
1976    "Syllable-Based Generalizations in English Phonology." Bloomington: Indiana U. Linguistics Club.
Kaufman, Stephen A.
1974    *The Akkadian Influences on Aramaic*. AS 19. Chicago: Oriental Institute.
Kaye, Jonathan
1975    "A Functional Explanation for Rule Ordering in Phonology." pp. 244-252. In Robin E. Grossman et al., eds. *Papers from the Parasession on Functionalism*. Chicago: Chicago Linguistic Society.

Kenstowicz, Michael and Kisseberth, Charles
  1979  *Generative Phonology: Description and Theory.* New York: Academic.
Kenstowicz, Michael J. and Pyle, Charles
  1973  "On the Phonological Integrity of Geminate Clusters." pp. 27-43. In Kenstowicz and C. W. Kisseberth, eds. *Issues in Phonological Theory.* Janua Linguarum, Series Maior 74. The Hague: Mouton.
Kienast, Burkhart
  1957  "Verbalformen mit Reduplikation im Akkadischen." *Or.* 26: 44-50.
  1960  *Die altassyrischen Texte des orientalischen Seminars der Universität Heidelberg und der Sammlung Erlenmeyer-Basel.* Berlin: W. de Gruyter.
King, Robert D.
  1969  *Historical Linguistics and Generative Grammar.* Englewood Cliffs: Prentice-Hall.
Kiparsky, Paul
  1968  "Metrics and Morphophonemics in the Kalevala." pp. 137-148. In Charles E. Gribble, ed. *Studies Presented to Professor Roman Jakobson by His Students.* Cambridge, MA: Slavica.
  1971a. [1965]. "Phonological Change." Bloomington: Indiana U. Linguistics Club.
  1971b. "Historical Linguistics." pp. 576-649. In William O. Dingwall, ed. *A Survey of Linguistic Science.* College Park: U. Of Maryland.
  1972a. "Metrics and Morphophonemics in the Rigveda." pp. 171-200. In Michael K. Brame, ed. *Contributions to Generative Phonology.* Austin: U. of Texas.
  1972b. "Explanation in Phonology." pp. 189-227. In Stanley Peters, ed. *Goals of Linguistic Theory.* Englewood Cliffs: Prentice-Hall.
  1973a. "Phonological Representations." pp. 1-136. In Osamu Fujimura, ed. *Three Dimensions of Linguistic Theory.* Tokyo: TEC.
  1973b. "The Role of Linguistics in a Theory of Poetry." *Daedalus* 102/3: 231-244.
  1973c. "'Elsewhere' in Phonology." pp. 93-106. In Stephen R. Anderson and P. Kiparsky, eds. *A Festschrift for Morris Halle.* New York: Holt, Rinehart and Winston.
  1975  "Stress, Syntax, and Meter." *Lang.* 51: 576-616.
Kisseberth, Charles W.
  1969  "On the Role of Derivational Constraints in Phonology." Bloomington: Indiana U. Linguistics Club.
  1970a. "On the Functional Unity of Phonological Rules." *LI* 1: 291-306.
  1970b. "Vowel Elision in Tonkawa and Derivational Constraints." pp. 109-137. In Jerrold M. Sadock and Anthony L. Vanek, eds. *Studies Presented to Robert B. Lees by His Students.* Champaign: U. of Illinois.
  1970c. "The Treatment of Exceptions." *Papers in Linguistics* 2: 44-58.
  1972  "On Derivative Properties of Phonological Rules." pp. 201-228. In Michael K. Brame, ed. *Contributions to Generative Phonology.* Austin: U. of Texas.
Knudsen, Ebbe E.
  1980  "Stress in Akkadian." *JCS* 32: 3-16.
Kraus, F. R.
  1976  "Der akkadische Vokativ." pp. 293-297. In Barry L. Eichler, ed. *Kramer Anniversary Volume.* *AOAT* 25. Kevelaer/Neukirchen-Vluyn: Butzon and Bercker/Neukirchener Verlag.
Kurylowicz, Jerzy
  1972  *Studies in Semitic Grammar and Metrics.* Wrocław: Polska Akademia Nauk.
Ladefoged, Peter
  1971  *Preliminaries to Linguistic Phonetics.* Chicago: Chicago U.
Lakoff, George
  1970  *Irregularity in Syntax.* New York: Holt, Rinehart & Winston.
Lambert, W. G.
  1969  Review of *Akkadisches Handwörterbuch* Fascicles 7 and 8 by W. von Soden. *JSS* 14: 247-251.

Landsberger, Benno
1965 [1928]. "Die Eigenbegrifflichkeit der babylonischen Welt: Ein Vortrag." Darustadt: Wissenschaftliche Buchgesellschaft.

Lehiste, Ilse
1970 *Suprasegmentals.* Cambridge: MIT.
1978 "The Syllable as a Structural Unit in Estonian." pp. 73-83. In A. Bell and J. B. Hooper, eds. *Syllables and Segments.* Amsterdam/New York: North-Holland.

Leslau, Wolf
1942 "South-East Semitic (Ethiopic and South Arabic)." *JAOS* 62: 4-14.

Lévi-Strauss, Claude
1970 "Overture to *Le cru et le cuit.*" pp. 31-55. In Jacques Ehrmann, ed. *Structuralism.* Garden City: Doubleday.

Lewy, Julius
1938 "Notes on Pre-Ḥurrian Texts from Nuzi." *JAOS* 58: 450-461.
1949 "Apropos of the Akkadian Numerals *iš-ti-a-na* and *iš-ti-na.*" *Ar. Or.* 17/2: 110-123.

Lieberman, Stephen J.
1977 *The Sumerian Loanwords in Old-Babylonian Akkadian, Volume One: Prolegomena and Evidence.* Missoula: Scholars.

Liberman, Mark and Prince, Alan
1977 "On Stress and Linguistic Rhythm." *LI* 8: 249-336.

Lisker, Leigh
1978 "Segment Duration, Voicing, and the Syllable." pp. 133-140. In A. Bell and J. B. Hooper, eds. *Syllables and Segments.* Amsterdam/New York: North-Holland.

Lord, Albert B.
1965 *The Singer of Tales.* New York: Atheneum.

Lowenstamm, Jean
1981 "On the Maximal Cluster Approach to Syllable Structure." *LI* 12: 575-604.

MacKay, Donald G.
1978 "Speech Errors inside the Syllable." pp. 201-212. In A. Bell and J. B. Hooper, eds. *Syllables and Segments.* Amsterdam/New York: North-Holland.

MacNeilage, Peter and Ladefoged, Peter
1976 "The Production of Speech and Language." pp. 75-120. In Edward C. Carterette and M. P. Friedman, eds. *Handbook of Perception, Volume VII: Language and Speech.* New York: Academic.

Malkiel, Yakov
1968a. *Essays on Linguistic Themes.* Oxford: Basil Blackwell.
1968b. "The Inflectional Paradigm as an Occasional Determinant of Sound Change." pp. 21-64. In W. P. Lehmann and Y. Malkiel, eds. *Directions for Historical Linguistics.* Austin: U. of Texas.

Malone, Joseph L.
1969 "Rules of Synchronic Analogy: A Proposal Based on Evidence from Three Semitic Languages." *Foundations of Language* 5: 534-559.
1971a. "Wave Theory, Rule Ordering, and Hebrew-Aramaic Segolation." *JAOS* 91: 44-66.
1971b. "Systematic Metathesis in Mandaic." *Lang.* 47: 394-415.
1975 "Systematic vs. Autonomous Phonemics and the Hebrew Grapheme *dagesh.*" *AAL* 2/7: 1-17.
1976 "Phonological Evidence for Syntactic Bracketing: A Surprise from Tiberian Hebrew." pp. 486-494. In S. S. Mufwene et al., eds. *Papers from the Twelfth Regional Meeting.* Chicago: Chicago Linguistic Society.
1979-80 "Semitic 'Internal Flexion' and Morphophonological Theory." pp. 88-102. In Edward Battistella, ed. *Proceedings of the New England Linguistic Society*, Part 2.

Martin, W. J.
1957 "Some Notes on the Imperative in the Semitic Languages." *RSO* 32/1: 315-319.

Mayer, Walter
    1971    *Untersuchungen zur Grammatik des Mittelassyrischen. AOAT* Sonderreihe 2. Neukirchen-Vluyn:
            Butzon and Bercker.
McCarthy, John J.
    1979    "On Stress and Syllabification." *LI* 10: 443-465.
McCawley, James D.
    1978    "Where You Can Shove Infixes." pp. 213-221. In A. Bell and J. B. Hooper, eds. *Syllables
            and Segments.* Amsterdam/New York: North-Holland.
Menn, Lisa
    1978    "Phonological Units in Beginning Speech." pp. 157-171. In A. Bell and J. B. Hooper, eds.
            *Syllables and Segments.* Amsterdam/New York: North-Holland.
Miller, D. Gary
    1977    "Language Change and Poetic Options." *Lang.* 53: 21-38.
Moran, William L.
    1978    Review of *Assyrian Royal Inscriptions* Volume 2 by A. K. Grayson. *BASOR* 230: 71-72.
Moscati, Sabatino (ed.)
    1969    *An Introduction to the Comparative Grammar of the Semitic Languages.* Wiesbaden: Otto
            Harrassowitz.
Nöldeke, Theodor
    1910    *Neue Beiträge zur semitischen Sprachwissenschaft.* Strassburg: Trübner.
Nougayrol, Jean
    1950    Review of *Old Babylonian Omen Texts* by A. Goetze. *JAOS* 70: 110-113.
O'Bryan, Margie
    1974    "The Interaction of Morphological and Phonological Processes in Historical Change."
            *Linguistics* 137: 49-61.
Ohsiek, Deborah
    1978    "Heavy Syllables and Stress." pp. 35-43. In A. Bell and J. B. Hooper, eds. *Syllables and
            Segments.* Amsterdam/New York: North-Holland.
O'Leary, De Lacy
    1969    *Comparative Grammar of the Semitic Languages.* Amsterdam: Philo.
Oppenheim, A. Leo et al.
    1955-   *The Assyrian Dictionary.* Chicago: Oriental Institute.
Parpola, Simo
    1974    "The Alleged Middle/Neo-Assyrian Irregular Verb *\*naṣṣ* and the Assyrian Sound Change š > s."
            *Assur* 1/1: 1-10.
Piaget, Jean
    1970    *Structuralism.* New York: Harper and Row.
Poebel, Arno
    1923    *Grundzüge der sumerische Grammatik.* Rostock: Rostocker orientalische Studien.
    1939    *Studies in Akkadian Grammar. AS* 9. Chicago: Oriental Institute.
Pyle, Charles
    1974    "Why a Conspiracy?" pp. 275-284. In Anthony Bruck et al., eds. *Papers from the Parasession
            on Natural Phonology.* Chicago: Chicago Linguistic Society.
Rainey, Anson F.
    1974    "Dust and Ashes." *Tel Aviv* 1: 77-83.
Ravn, O. E.
    1949    "Babylonian Permansive and Status Indeterminatus." *Ar. Or.* 17/1: 300-306.
Reiner, Erica
    1964    "The Phonological Interpretation of a Subsystem in the Akkadian Syllabary." pp. 167-180.
            *Studies Presented to A. Leo Oppenheim.* Chicago: Oriental Institute.
    1966    *A Linguistic Analysis of Akkadian.* Janua Linguarum, Series Practica 21. The Hague: Mouton.
    1970    "Akkadian." pp. 274-303. In *Current Trends in Linguistics* 6. The Hague: Mouton.

1973a. "How We Read Cuneiform Texts." *JCS* 25:3-58.

1973b. "New Cases of Morphophonemic Spellings." *Or.* 42: 35-38.

Reiner, Erica with Pingree, David

1975    *Babylonian Planetary Omens, Part One.* Bibliotheca Mesopotamica 2/1. Malibu: Undena.

Renger, J.

1972    Review of *Grundriss der akkadischen Grammatik* by W. von Soden. *JNES* 31: 228-232.

Riemschneider, Kaspar K.

1976    "Compound Graphemic Units in Standard Babylonian Cuneiform Writing." *JCS* 28: 65-71.

Rimalt, E. S.

1933/34 "Zur Lautlehre des Neubabylonischen." *AfO* 9: 124-126.

Rodgers, Jonathan H.

1977    "Semitic Accentual Systems." Yale U.: Ph.D. dissertation.

Rowton, Michael B.

1962    "The Use of the Permansive in Classic Babylonian." *JNES* 21: 233-303

Rudes, Blair A.

1977    "Another Look at Syllable Structure." Bloomington: Indiana U. Linguistics Club.

Ryckmans, G.

1938    *Grammaire accadienne.* Louvain: Bureaux du Muséon.

Saib, Jilali

1978    "Segment Organization and the Syllable in Tamazight Berber." pp. 93-104. In A. Bell and J. B. Hooper, eds. *Syllables and Segments.* Amsterdam/New York: North-Holland.

Salonen, Armas

1949    "Notes on the Stem R-K-B in Akkadian." *Ar. Or.* 17/2: 313-322.

Saporta, Sol

1965    "Ordered Rules, Dialect Differences, and Historical Processes." *Lang.* 41-218-224.

Sarauw, Chr.

1939    *Über Akzent und Silbenbildung in dem älteren semitischen Sprachen.* Copenhagen: Einar Munksgaard.

Schane, Sanford A.

1972    "Natural Rules in Phonology." pp. 199-229. In Robert P. Stockwell and Ronald K. S. Macauley, eds. *Linguistic Change and Generative Theory.* Bloomington: Indiana U.

1973a. *Generative Phonology.* Englewood Cliffs: Prentice-Hall.

1973b. "The Treatment of Phonological Exceptions: The Evidence from French." pp. 822-835. In Braj B. Bachru et al., eds. *Issues in Linguistics.* Urbana: U. of Illinois.

Schane, Sanford A. et al.

1974/75 "On the Psychological Reality of a Natural Rule of Syllable Structure." *Cognition* 3: 351-358.

Schileico, Woldemar

1928/29 "Ein babylonischer Weihtext in griechischer Schrift." *AfO* 5: 11-13.

Sekine, Masao

1973    "The Subdivisions of the North-West Semitic Languages." *JSS* 18: 205-221.

Shibatani, Masayoshi

1973    "The Role of Surface Phonetic Constraints in Generative Phonology." *Lang.* 49: 87-106.

Sievers, E.

1929    "Beiträge zur babylonischen Metrik." *ZA* 4: 1-38.

von Soden, Wolfram

1932-33 "Der hymnisch-epische Dialekt des Akkadischen." *ZA* 40: 163-227; 41: 90-183.

1950    "Ein Zweigespräch Ḫammurabis mit einer Frau." *ZA* 15: 151-194.

1958-81 *Akkadisches Handwörterbuch.* Wiesbaden: Otto Harrassowitz.

1969    *Grundriss der akkadischen Grammatik. An. Or.* 33/47. Rome: Pontifical Biblical Institute.

1970    Review of *Sequential Reconstruction of Proto-Akkadian* by I. J. Gelb. *JNES* 29: 202-207.

Sommerstein, Alan H.

    1974    "On Phonotactically Motivated Rules." *Journal of Linguistics* 10: 71-94.

    1977    *Modern Phonology.* Baltimore: University Park.

Speiser, E. A.

    1941    *Introduction to Hurrian. AASOR.* New Haven: American Schools for Oriental Research.

    1953    "Comments on Recent Studies in Akkadian Grammar." *JAOS* 73: 129-138.

    1967    *Oriental and Biblical Studies.* Ed. by Jacob J. Finkelstein and Moshe Greenberg. Philadelphia: U. of Pennsylvania.

Steiner, Richard C.

    1974    "Rule Split, Rule Loss, and Alternational Flip-Flop: The True Story of a Proto-Semitic Syncope Rule in Hebrew, Arabic, and Akkadian." Unpublished paper presented at the Third North American Conference on Semitic [now Afroasiatic] Linguistics.

    1976    "On the Origin of the ḥéðɛr ~ haðár Alternation in Hebrew." *AAL* 3/5: 1-18.

    1979    "From Proto-Hebrew to Mishnaic Hebrew: The History of יֶ֫ךָ and קֶ֫ךָ ." *Hebrew Annual Review* 3: 157-174.

    1980    "Yuqaṭṭil, Yaqaṭṭil, or Yiqaṭṭil: D-Stem Prefix-Vowels and a Constraint on Reduction in Hebrew and Aramaic." *JAOS* 100: 513-518.

Ungnad, Arthur

    1903    "Zur Syntax der Gesetze Hammurabis." *ZA* 17: 353-378.

    1923    "Auslautende Explosivlaute im Sumerischen." *OLZ*: 424-426.

Ungnad, Arthur and Matouš, Lubor

    1969    *Grammatik des Akkadischen.* 5th rev. ed. Munich: Beck.

Vennemann, Theo

    1972a.    "On the Theory of Syllabic Phonology." *Linguistische Berichte* 18: 1-18.

    1972b.    "Phonetic Detail in Assimilation: Problems in Germanic Phonology." *Lang.* 48: 863-892.

    1974    "Words and Syllables." pp. 346-374. In Anthony Bruck et al., eds. *Papers from the Parasession on Natural Phonology.* Chicago: Chicago Linguistic Society.

Wang, William S.-Y.

    1964    "Phonological Features of Tone." *International Journal of American Linguistics* 33: 93-105.

Wevers, John W.

    1969    Review of *A Linguistic Analysis of Akkadian* by E. Reiner. *JNES* 28: 290-292.

Whiting, Robert M.

    1981    "The R Stem(s) in Akkadian." *Or.* 50: 1-39.

Ylvisaker, Sigurd C.

    1912    *Zur babylonischen und assyrischen Grammatik.* Leipziger semitische Studien 5/6.

Zimmern, H.

    1890    "Zur assyrischen und vergleichenden semitischen Lautlehre." *ZA* 5: 367-398.

# PREDICATIVE STATE AND INFLECTION OF THE NOMINAL PREDICATE IN AKKADIAN AND SYRIAC

## Amikam Gai

### The Hebrew University, Jerusalem

In his article "An Interpretation of the Akkadian Stative as a Nominal sentence," G. Buccellati (1968) argues for the statement expressed by the title of his article, and for recognizing the stative as a noun in a special state, namely, the 'predicative state.' Almost at the end of this article (page 11, 4 lines from bottom) he writes ". . . that Akkadian seems to be the only Semitic language . . . to be endowed with a special state for the noun when this serves as predicate." The present article is written as a response to this statement.

Buccellati's main purpose in this article is to shatter the conception that the stative is a tense, or any kind of verbal form; its description must be undertaken in the framework of the noun, particularly its syntax. This intention cannot be over-welcomed. However, in Buccellati's great zeal to prove this thesis, he does not leave enough room to study the differences between this type of nominal sentence and others. Thus, the uniqueness of that phenomenon (in the framework of the noun-syntax), although expressed, is not, in my opinion, sufficiently emphasized. It is convenient and adequate to follow Buccellati's description of the situation in Akkadian, but some remarks and modifications are needed mainly for placing a different emphasis on his points.

The noun in Akkadian, when serving as a predicate (and not "immediately followed by a qualification or complement, or by the particle -ma"; Buccellati p. 7 in the middle) has two characteristics. (1) It appears in a special state. (2) It inflects by taking a specific set of endings, which express gender and number, for rendering the subject; the ending may or may not have a nominal apposition; the 3rd person sg.m. ending is $\emptyset$. These characteristics are true for every noun acting as a predicate, although most frequently these endings are found with the element known as 'verbal adjective.' This phenomenon is called 'stative,' and it is a *sui generis* way of adding a copula to the nominal sentence of that pattern; as for the pattern, it demands a copula.

These two characteristics determine a unique status for this type of nominal sentence, which distinguishes it not only from the common Semitic nominal sentence (e.e. Hebrew, Arabic, Ge'ez or Biblical Aramaic), but also from its Akkadian counterpart *etlum muttallum anāku* (Buccellati, p. 11 line 1), which has neither of these characteristics.

A purely synchronical investigation of Syriac, clear of historical or etymological sediments, reveals a similar picture. (1) The adjective (including participle) serving as a predicate, appears in a special state, that known as 'status absolutus' (whereas, when acting as an attribute or in any other syntactic position, it appears in the common state, that known as 'status emphaticus') (See Nöldeke (1904) §204A.) (2) Every nominal predicate (as a whole, not only the adjective) is accompanied, as a rule, by a copula, and it is normally carried out that way: The noun in that syntactic position inflects, taking what is to be considered in that stage of the language, as a special set of suffixes rendering its subject; the ending may or may not have a nominal apposition. Diachronically speaking, these endings are (mostly) shortened forms of the pronouns. (See Nöldeke (1904) §§64 and 311.) The picture is completely identical with Akkadian in the case of a participle acting as a predicate, as the 3rd person sg. m. ending in $\emptyset$. (See Duval (1881) §183.)

These two parallel phenomena existed in two different languages, in different periods, and have no common etymological origin. However, it is interesting to note (particularly when one remembers that the situation described here for Syriac is similar in other contemporary eastern Aramaic dialects as well, e.g. Mandaic or Aramaic of the Babylonian Talmud),[1] that these two phenomena took place in the same geographical areas in a more or less continuous course of time.

## REFERENCES

Buccellati G. (1968) "An Interpretation of the Akkadian Stative as a Nominal Sentence" *JNES* 27: 1-12.
Duval R. (1881) *Traité de grammaire syriaque,* Paris.
Nöldeke Th. (1904) *Compendious Syriac Grammar* (translated by J. A. Crichton) London.

[1] The western (Palestinian) dialects viz. Galilean Aramaic, Palestinian Christian Aramaic, and Samaritan Aramaic differ in both points. (1) A status absolutus in the predicative adjective cannot be considered as 'predicative state,' for in these dialects the two states are (still?) used to distinguish states of determination. (2) The nominal sentence does not demand a copula.